Authentic Hope, Possessing the Unfo

M000223844

Author: Arnold J. Allen
Publisher: Increase Hope Foundation, February 2016
www.IncreaseHope.com

The power of authentic hope is viewed from a living relationship with a real God and real people. With the understanding of the eternal, transcendent activity of hope, Arnold applies truth and life of the Spirit of God to everyday life. Whether in favor and confidence or grief and loss, authentic hope pulls toward a future filled with promise and destiny. Hope is described from the perspective of psychology, biology and spirituality. Gaining insight into the resources of hope in body, soul and spirit, the reader is challenged to position the heart toward partnering with the God of all hope. In discovering an energy of hope that matches the effects of morphine or the strength of spirit to avoid suicide, hope is illustrated by real life stories of defeat and victory.

Guidance in practical, effective activities for fostering hope in others as well as maintaining a hope-filled lifestyle equips the reader to co-create a promising future. Whether dealing with hope deferred or understanding the partnership of faith, hope and love, this fresh look at authentic hope will be especially helpful to those wanting to strengthen their foundation in this Biblical truth.

# Authentic Hope

## Possessing The Unfolding Future

# Endorsements

In his book, *Authentic Hope*, Arnold Allen beautifully and thoughtfully makes the case for the essential nature of hope. He leaves no stone unturned as he navigates the reader through scripture to reveal hope's power to transform every aspect of life. To read *Authentic Hope* is to become convinced that hope is not only the message for this season, but the message for all time.

David Crone, Senior Leader

The Mission, Vacaville, CA - www.missionvacaville.org

Author of *The Power of Your Life Message: Decisions That Define Us, Declarations that Empower Us,* and *Prisoner of Hope: Captivated by the Expectation of Good.*

\* \* \* \* \*

Hope is not a positive attitude or wishful thinking. Hope is a reality. Most of the time our culture devalues hope and down plays it to wishing. Arnold helps put hope back in its rightful place so it awakens hearts to the goodness of God. This book provides a needed focus on a vital topic.

Eric Reeder

RISE movement: A global movement of hope

www.generationsrise.com

\* \* \* \* \*

Hope is not a well understood concept; probably neglected by theologians over generations. Hope—relational hope—is truly God's idea, and is provided to us to help us focus on our future and eternal hope. Author Arnold Allen has gone beyond just simple theology, writing in depth on the importance of biblical hope and its practical application for our health and healing. My hope—my true expectation—is that the reader of this excellently written work will experience greater hope in all God has affirmed to us as believers in His word.

Stan E. DeKoven, Ph.D., MFT

Founder and President

Vision International University www.vision.edu

International Training and Education Network


* * * * *

Everyone needs hope; it is God's promise. He gives it to us in scripture in many ways, telling us even when things are difficult, there is hope, the light at the end of the tunnel. Arnold Allen understands how the hope of Christ works in your life. This book will take you through the steps, stages, and seasons of life and show you how you can live with hope in every trial and every victory.

Loren Cunningham, Founder

Youth With A Mission (YWAM) - www.YWAM.org


* * * * *

I have always been comforted and encouraged by the scripture Arnold Allen has used to set the stage for his book: *Authentic Hope.* (Genesis 9:13) As we look about us today, we can clearly see the fading hope of millions. Reading Arnold's book has stirred my heart to look carefully to that which I base my hope on for the future. It cannot be the Rainbow itself, it must be the Source of the Rainbow, Jesus Christ. God clearly had the desire to instill hope in Noah and the future of the ages to come. Arnold has given us such a good and clear picture of not only the need for Hope in these days, but how very important this whole subject is. Reading the passage in Genesis 9:13 brings together even more clearly the message brought to us in this book.

Lorrie White

Walnut Grove, B.C., Canada

(Widow of Dr. John White)

\* \* \* \* \*

The content of the book is fantastic and much needed.

Dr. Bob Nichols, PhD

Changing Hearts, Changing Lives Ministry

www.DrBobNichols.com

Thanks for tackling a needed subject to explore. I love the interaction of spirit to spirit and spirit to environment. I had fun with the reading of this. It's a spirit-inspiring chapter. Hope not deferred,

Rob Mazza
Destiny Workshops
Dalton Gardens, ID


* * * * *


For many years the church has not excelled in teaching the difference between faith and hope. The concept of biblical hope has not often been preached from our pulpits. As a result there has been confusion about this issue. Many generations of Christians have not learned to live life out of a sense of biblical hope. This book clarifies the concept of hope and how to live life with that concept as a central facet of one's life. It teaches how to live in hope even in the face of negative and challenging life events. The author is an engaging writer. He incorporates a solid understanding of scripture along with many real-life examples and stories. The stories help the reader to apply the concepts taught in the book. I recommend this book to all people who want a better understanding of how to live in hope.

Catherine Skillin, PsyD, RP, RMFT
Major, The Salvation Army
Director of Counseling Services


* * * * *

Hope gives peace and joy. Arnold's book is a shining example of how hope can transform a person's life.

Kathryn Parslow, PhD
Certified Clinical Nutritionist
Author of *Surviving the American High-Tech Diet*

* * * * *

Although I have read many books on the topic of HOPE and have had many interesting discussions with many HOPE experts I found gems in this book that I have found nowhere else. Arnold writes in a way that the reader wants to keep on reading—he is a master storyteller and his stories anchor his research and his experiences. Linking Hope to intuition, emotion, the intellect, creativity and energy just opens up a new understanding of this elusive concept. Unpacking Hope as a mind and heart process and state was indeed revealing—Arnold's approach is fresh and original. I loved reading this book and I recommend it strongly to everyone —and I mean everyone. We cannot live without this kind of Hope.

Dr. Kobus Neethling
President of the South African Creativity Foundation
Author of more than 90 international best-sellers.
Creator of over 25 Neethling Brain Instruments
www.KobusNeethling.com

* * * * *

# Authentic Hope

## Possessing The Unfolding Future

*by*

## Arnold J. Allen

*Published by*

**Increase Hope Foundation**

www.IncreaseHope.com

Bellingham, Washington

# Dedication

This book is dedicated to two of the many amazing women in my life. Truly women of authentic hope!

To my mother, Hazel May (Hurst) Allen, in heaven now, who demonstrated the love of life and enduring hope in her journey.

To Carol Lynne (Knepper) Allen, my wife of 45 years—this book is as much your journey as mine. Your belief in me as a 'hope messenger' has inspired my endurance more than any other!

The spiritual DNA of these women of authentic hope will be manifest for generations of natural and spiritual children.

# Acknowledgements

I want to express my appreciation for the many whom have supported Carol and me in this book-writing journey. Spiritual mentors, faithful (and hopeful!) intercessors and prophetic voices, family, friends, colleagues, and those giving me writing space, especially the folks at Methow Valley Ranch in Winthrop for my first manuscript and Debbie Okon at the Liberty House in Bellingham! Thanks to the community of Abundant Life Church, especially Ted and Bonnie Hanson!

Special thanks to Jim Bryson for your editorial work and the tutoring! Thank you, Emilyanne Zornes, for loving me and my work while proofing the script. Thank you to Claudia Santiago and VPGI Enterprises team for helping to establish the necessary roadmap and systems for Increase Hope Foundation and handling the publishing and marketing of the book. Thank you to Jacque Peterson for a final polishing of the manuscript. A special thank you to my daughter, Amani Hanson, for the cover and art work! Your love and encouragement has been a sustaining force on the journey.

Thank you to the critical readers, especially Cathy Cleveland, Jen Washtock and Catherine Madera. Your fingerprints are numerous. Thank you to the many friends that have graciously allowed me to share their stories so others may have hope. Special thanks to you Henry! You have inspired me to hope in the very most difficult season of my life. Your story will serve as a beacon in the fog of pain for others, as it has for me.

I appreciate the investment of the various folks for endorsements.

As a symbol of safety, confidence and certainty, early Christians adopted the anchor as a symbol of hope. It ranks among the most ancient of symbols relating to the virtue of hope of salvation and holding secure in faith. Anchors are found in many inscriptions in the catacombs of Rome. As a symbol of hope, they were often carved on gems. Hope in Christ was seen as the soul's anchor. Increase Hope Foundation uses the anchor symbol as a reminder of the earliest hope-filled followers of Christ and our present confidence in his sustaining power

*We who have fled to him for refuge can have great confidence as we hold to the hope that lies before us. This hope is a strong and trustworthy anchor for our souls. It leads us through the curtain into God's inner sanctuary.*

Hebrews 6:18b-19 (NLT)

# Contents

# Authentic Hope
## Possessing The Unfolding Future
www.AuthenticHopeBook.com / www.IncreaseHope.com

Copyright © 2016 Arnold J. Allen
ISBN: 978-0-9828255-0-1

Bible translations used: King James Version (KJV) Public Domain. New King James Version (NKJV) Copyright 1982 Thomas Nelson, Inc. Nashville, TN. New American Standard Bible (NASB) 1995 by The Lockman Foundation, La Habra, CA. New Century Version (NCV): Worthy Publishing, Ft. Worth, TX. Message Bible (MSG) Eugene H. Peterson, Navpress Publishing, Colorado Springs, CO. New International Version (NIV) Zondervan Publishing House, Grand Rapids, Mi. Amplified Bible (AMP) Zondervan Publishing House, Grand Rapids, MI. New Living Translation (NLT) 1996 Tyndale House Foundation, Carol Stream, IL. Contemporary English Version (CEV) American Bible Society New York, NY.

Personal stories used with permission, or names and story details have been changed.

Editing: Jim Bryson (JamesLBryson@gmail.com)
Proofing: Emily-Anne Zornes (Em.Zornes@yahoo.com)
Typesetting: Jacque Peterson (jacque@macaddicts.net)
Art & Design: Amani Hanson, Becoming Studios
Author's Photo: Jessica Drake Photography
Publishing Agent - Editing - Marketing - PR:
    Claudia Santiago (www.VPGroupinternational.com / www.ClaudiaSantiago.com)

Excerpt(s) from THE ANATOMY OF HOPE: HOW PEOPLE PREVAIL IN THE FACE OF ILLNESS by Jerome Groopman, copyright © 2003 by Jerome Groopman. Used by permission of Random House, an imprint and division of Penguin Random House LLC. Any third party use of this material, outside of this publication, is prohibited. Interested parties must apply directly to Penguin Random House LLC for permission. All rights reserved.

Cherie Calbom, The Juice Lady's Remedies for Stress and Adrenal Fatigue (Lake Mary, FL: Siloam, 2014), Used by permission.

# Foreword

## by Harold Eberle

www.WorldCastMinistries.com

Before reading Arnold J. Allen's book, I thought I had a good understanding of hope, but I was wrong! My friend, Arnold, introduces us to an overlooked power. I, along with many Christians, had emphasized love and faith to the degree that we minimized the role of hope. As Arnold explains, we saw hope as "the weaker alternative" to love and faith. We pushed hope aside and went after what we considered the more important characteristics of love and faith.

As Arnold explains clearly, hope is not a second class, weak version of faith. Some of Arnold's most clarifying statements include these:

*"Hope, by design, moves toward a given destination."*
*"Hope has the power to change our lives."*
*"Authentic, spiritual hope is a dynamic part of the living, innate energy harnessing the physical, mental and emotional elements of our nature as we move into the unfolding future."*

It was not until I read over halfway through Arnold's insightful book that I realized how limited my understanding of hope had been. Gradually, then suddenly, I found myself embracing hope. Allowing hope to explode in me. Allowing hope to produce its work: to carry me, to heal me, to empower me. I realized how I am created by God to ride hope into the future. Then and only then will hope open doors before me. Then and only then will I catch the hope-filled wind that blows from God's throne room 24 hours a day, everyday.

Thank you Arnold, for helping me see the value of a hope-filled life.

Restorative hope is the answer to people when their deepest desires are crushed and treachery has stolen their future.

*"I have set my rainbow in the clouds, and it will be the sign of the covenant between me and the earth."*

Genesis 9:13 (NIV)

# Introduction
# Chasing Rainbows

## Catching Hope

I grew up part of a large family in the mountains of northern Vermont; a place of stunning imagery and violent thunderstorms. As a child, the best thing about these sky-splitting cataclysms was the rainbows appearing at the end. My siblings and I would watch the colors touch the earth, and with a cry of joy, we'd race to the spot bearing the pot of gold. But no matter how well we ran, the rainbow always drifted away before we reached it. I can remember shouting instructions from the porch to guide my brother to ground zero. Once I actually saw my sister standing in the dazzling colors—she had found it!—yet sadly no gold. Today I no longer chase rainbows, but I still enjoy their beauty and revel in their significant meaning.

Since Biblical times, the rainbow has been a symbol of hope, attached not to a mystical pot of gold but to the absolute nature and character of God. As a sign of His faithfulness and future fulfillment of promises, the bow in the sky reminds us that He is watching over us with favor.

*This is the sign of the covenant I am making between me and you and everything living around you and everyone living after you. I am putting my rainbow in the clouds, a sign of the covenant between me and the Earth. From now on, when I form a cloud over the Earth and the rainbow appears in the cloud, I'll remember my covenant between me and you and every living thing, that never again will floodwaters destroy all life.*

Genesis 9:12-16 (MSG)

He is a God of hope and promise. Because we are His offspring, this same sense of future fulfillment of promises and eternity has been fashioned into our nature. God is expectant; we are expectant!

## The Weaker Link?

Hope, faith and love form an eternal trinity of heavenly qualities intended for an earthly purpose:

*But for right now, until that completeness, we have three things to do to lead us toward that consummation: Trust steadily (faith) in God, hope unswervingly, love extravagantly.*

1 Corinthians 13:13 (MSG)

## Faith and Love

Much has been written throughout history about faith and love. Today, there are faith movements, words of faith and heroes of the faith. Thousands of sermons, preached weekly around the world, inspire us to greater faith. Along with faith, the pursuit and attainment of love is celebrated from Shakespeare's sonnets to Sunday pulpits. Love is the central theme in countless songs, books and films from the secular to the sacred. There is no denying the human craving for love. We seek it from birth, pursue it amid the trials and joys of life, and yearn for a love-filled hereafter.

Certainly, faith and love are important, but we have to ask: What about hope? All too often, it seems like hope is the weaker alternative. For many, hope remains an elusive concept. We may glimpse its color from time to time, but the sense of promise is as elusive as the mystical treasure. Experience forges the misguided virtue of hoping for the best while fearing the worst. Hope is on par with wishful thinking—a weak link unable to bear the pressure of real life. But is this the true nature of hope? Or is there a power in hope that is more than a wish, greater than a fleeting fantasy? If so, what does authentic hope look like and how may it be fleshed out in the realities of life? Clearly, faith and love are understood by people in the context of relationship to God and one another. Is there a relational aspect to hope? Does the fuller concept of hope share the importance of faith and love? Although hope is about the future, how does one see the rainbow and dance in the passing rain?

Because of this future dimension, hope is central to the existence of mankind. After all, life is more about the future than the past. Just as the rainbow is the sun shining through the storm, hopeful expectation of the future draws us into each new day. Hope is a future-oriented determination, an attitude of the heart, and a promise of relationships. Just as it is impossible to define human beings without describing life, it is impossible to describe life without including hope. Hope is knowing the sun will rise tomorrow. The endless rhythm of the waves washing the beach affirms our sense of future. In hope, we conceive children, compose music, write books and plant vineyards. Hope becomes our anticipated "yet to come". Hope is the vigor in the grape seed bearing the blueprint of the plant—the promised future. Hope is the idea, the energy and the passion that creates tomorrow. Enlarged through waiting, hope is the womb in which faith and love increase, flourish and have their fullest expression.

Despite its deep nature, the concept of hope has lost its meaning as originally intended in Scripture. It has become a vague idea, a wish or fantasy. It is our whimsical reason for buying a lottery ticket or dropping chips on RED 7. Yet, when I tell people that I am devoted to strengthening hope in others, nearly every person replies, *"We really need hope!"* The instinctual understanding that hope is essential resonates with the core of our being. Trust, engagement, accountability, adaptability to change, and creativity are all born from authentic, wholehearted hope. We need to rethink and redefine hope. Our definition and experience must demonstrate the authenticity of innate, wholehearted hope.

It is important to look at some viewpoints from Scripture, as well as physiological and psychological perspectives in defining and experiencing hope. We will come to learn that well beyond positive thinking or wishing on a star, or even the elusive pot of gold, hope energizes life with an expectation of favor, confidence and anticipation.

Examining the Biblical viewpoint, the relationship between hope and faith will be considered, as well as practical life applications. We will think through the questions: *Does hope grow up and become faith? Or are we only treading water when we exercise hope and not faith? Is hope only future or does it find expression in the here and now?* Hope, as characterized in the original Biblical language, carries the idea of confident waiting for the object of our trust:

> *For we were saved in this hope, but hope that is seen is not hope; for why does one still hope for what he sees? But if we hope for what we do not see, we eagerly wait for it with perseverance.*

> Romans 8:24-25 (NKJV)

Proverbs tells us:

> *Hope deferred makes the heart sick, but desire fulfilled is a tree of life.*

> Proverbs 13:12 (NASB)

So if hope was only a weak sister to the other two virtues of faith and love, why does even its deferment make the recipient ill? How does its presence restore inactive brain waves of a comatose patient? Obviously, something more intrinsic to our nature is at work here.

Restorative hope is the answer to people when their deepest desires are crushed and treachery has stolen their future. For a broken humanity, hope is a function of struggle. Hope is the energy to grasp the unfolding future while limping from past wounds. Hope is the tree of life.

The key to authentic hope, as we will learn through our exploration, is relationship. We will look at the power of hope, including its influence on the physical body as strong as morphine yet as resilient as the life of God. The idea that a relational God created a relational people will be explored, along with insight on creating and nurturing a prevailing hope.

## From the Bible to American Idol

American Idol winner Danny Gokey sings about hope in his 2014 #1 hit *"Hope in Front of Me".* Danny performed in 2008, during the eighth season of the popular show where ordinary contestants cling to the desire that their talent will be discovered while competing in front of a panel of judges. In the final judging, he placed third and subsequently signed with a recording company in Nashville. Now that is the power of hope!

Witnessing the effort of an average Joe to break into the entertainment industry generates a lot of hope filled passion. What is notable about Danny's performance is not just his win or musical talent, but the fact that he performed just weeks after losing his wife, Sophia Martinez, during surgery to reverse congenital heart disease. Devastated by the loss, Gokey wanted to back out of the show, and finally agreed to go forward because it was Sophia's idea and desire for him. So what sustained Danny through this devastating loss, grief and the rebuilding of his private life? Here's Danny:

When you have no hope, life gets very difficult to live. I faced that! I didn't want to live. I fought through the tears. I fought through self-doubt. I fought anger and depression. I thought in the back of my mind, maybe something good can come out of the show. I felt that even in this difficult situation, good can come out of it. That is what was happening for me. I was going through the grieving process. It was a bitter-sweet place. [American Idol] became a point of hope in front of me. (Interview with Sister Rose at patheos.com)

We get a glimpse of his personal rainbow through his lyrics as he sings of the hope as light. With his heart looking beyond the horizon, hope pulls him forward. Danny connects us with the sense of being held while wanting to believe.

Danny, now remarried, has continued to flourish in his hope inspired journey and has started a foundation to bring hope and help to others. He was nominated for the New Artist of the Year Award (2015) by the Gospel Music Association. Danny's reflection, "God writes our story. Sometimes we have to let go of our plan to allow God's plan to take place."

Another American Idol winner, Chris Daughtry, sings about hope in his 2013 song *Undefeated*. Like Danny, Chris is a Christian in a secular industry. Unlike Danny, Chris' image of hope is a bit more gritty. He sings of the aftermath of a battle where the victor stands bruised and bleeding, yet with hope unbowed, unbroken.

As these artists show us, hope is not a vague fantasy or wishful thinking that stakes everything on an imagined pot of gold.

Hope is attached to something secure—*Someone* secure. This is relationally focused hope—a force that is in everyone and available to everyone. This is *dance-in-the-rain authentic hope*. And hope never dances alone. As they say in Texas, "You gotta' dance with who brung ya!" Hope always pulls us into the unfolding future.

We were breathed into existence with an attachment to the "yet to come." The reality of an eternal future is a natural condition for all human beings.

*He has made everything beautiful in its time. He has also set eternity in the human heart...*

Ecclesiastes 3:11 (NIV)

# 1
# Eternity Within

A Crafted Hope for Generations

## A journey of hope and healing

Sometimes tragedy or illness act like emotional Velcro for the pain of past experiences. Hope has a way of altering that Velcro experience. My friend Cherie Calbom has an amazing story of hope. Author of over 20 books in the field of nutrition, and along with her Orthodox priest husband Father John, she is an effective healing retreat presenter. But success has not come easy for Cherie, nor has life been without its cruel turns. The soul has incredible resilience even under the weight of great loss. Cherie has had more than her share of pain. Her brother died when she was two. Her mother succumbed to cancer when she was six years old. Some memories are vague but powerful, since she fainted at the funeral. Cherie went to live with her grandparents. The pain of losing her grandpa only three years later was beyond measure.

A few years later, her father became involved in a tragic

situation that took him from her daily life. As a teenager, Cherie experienced the pain, condemnation and struggle of eating disorders. Seeking to medicate the pain of so much loss and trauma, she found comfort to be elusive. Slowly, over the years, the spiritual and emotional pain found its fuller expression in her body. Chronic fatigue syndrome and fibromyalgia consumed her energy. At thirty, Cherie had to quit her job and move in with her father. As her body struggled with sickness and her soul grew heavy with grief and loss, her spirit managed a flame of hope. At times, it felt more like a "smoldering wick" than a flame of life. Perpetual lethargy, sluggishness and fever were the daily physical status. "Will I ever feel alive again? Will I spend my life in sickness?"

Without answers from the medical community, Cherie mustered enough energy to begin the search for healing on her own. Visiting various health food stores and libraries, and talking to anyone who seemed knowledgeable, she decided to give fresh juicing a try. Her great desire to be well made whole foods and fresh juice become her daily routine. Days turned to weeks and months as she sought to turn her life around. At times, her dad thought her eating routine would do her in. Cherie was determined to live. Although the pain of detoxing made wellness seem like an elusive dream, a hidden strength was forming.

Cherie said, "One day I woke up feeling different. I thought, "Maybe I'll go for a run today!" I just felt better. From that day on I knew things would get better, and they did!" The juice/ whole food diet coupled with the power of healing prayer brought the much-sought transformation. Cherie then returned to southern California with hopes to complete her first book. But the promising journey became abruptly interrupted.

## From Life to Death and Back

While house-sitting for friends on the July 4<sup>th</sup> holiday, Cherie was brutally assaulted. As she described the senseless attack, it seemed almost too bizarre. Awakened at 3:00 a.m., she was attacked by a pipe wielding intruder. She fought him off as he yelled, "Now you are dead!" He dropped the pipe and began choking her to unconsciousness. She recounts:

> I felt life leaving my body. I knew that I was dying. I felt my spirit leave in a sensation of popping out of my body and floating upward. Suddenly everything was peaceful and still. I sensed I was traveling, at what seemed like the speed of light, through black space. I saw what looked like lights twinkling in the distance. But all of a sudden I was back in my body, outside the house, clinging to a fence at the end of the dog run. I don't know how I got there. I screamed for help with all the breath I had. On my third scream, I thought that it was my last. Finally, the neighbor heard me and came to help.

The hope that sustained Cherie through the long journey of recovery from chronic fatigue syndrome and fibromyalgia was now needed more than ever. The physical injuries were numerous and very critical. Many months of surgeries and therapy, partnered with healing prayer, brought near complete restoration. It was truly miraculous. The emotional restoration however, took longer.

The terrorizing fear and anxiety were disabling. Trauma of physical injury, trauma of memories and emotions, trauma of childhood losses all partnered to imprison Cherie's spirit. As we sat at her kitchen table, Cherie described experiencing healing from the painful memories and trauma of the attack and the wounds from the past through prayer, laying on of hands and deep emotional healing work. Aspects of her own hope-filled healing journey are now part of the healing that she offers to others. Forgiveness, releasing pain, purging toxic emotions and receiving healing love have brought about complete restoration. Cherie is embracing the unfolding future with peace and confidence.

## Hope Season

In my American upbringing, the Christmas season heralded wonderful expectations of family gatherings, gift exchanges, feasts, and celebrations in worship and song. With nine siblings, our home was usually the hub of activity, and the holiday season kicked it into overdrive. Christmas created in all of us an excited anticipation of tables laden with food, surprise packages under the tree, and especially good will from my brothers and sisters.

But sometimes, although careful preparations were under-taken, our expectations did not work out the way we hoped. Whether it was trudging through the snow searching in vain for the perfect tree, scouring a crowded mall for an ideal gift, or struggling to roast a turkey that could make Julia Child cheer, failures and disappointments were bound to happen - indeed, they were inevitable. Some of our expectations were so high, nothing could possibly reach those lofty ideals. Still, it was the hope of greater things that energized our hectic activities.

How true of life in general. Every event or relationship for which we have high expectations can also carry great disappointments—as with Danny and the death of his young wife. It is the risk we take to hope, to dream, to reach for something better than we have today.

## Autumn—A Fashioned Gift

One Christmas day, six-year-old Autumn bolted from her room, filling the air with anguished sobs as she buried her face in her mother's lap. What could have possibly turned such a happy day into so much grief, her mother wondered? An hour earlier, a delighted Autumn was opening her presents with her siblings in front of a crackling fireplace. The aroma of mulled cider, fresh-baked cinnamon rolls and brewing coffee swirled in the air as the children reveled in their gifts.

But later, in the privacy of her bedroom, Autumn's frustration broke into tears as she struggled to get a new set of handmade doll clothes to fit her doll. Try as she might, the new wardrobe— her favorite gift that morning—did not fit. Oh the humanity! Her mother's efforts to console the distraught child were to no avail. All was lost, Christmas was ruined, and a lifetime of despair would surely follow. Or so it seemed to this little girl as she viewed life as a six-year-old.

So what led up to Autumn's moment of crushing disappointment? Months in advance, my wife Carol knew that our granddaughter would be receiving a new doll for Christmas. So Carol, a talented seamstress, began to sew clothes for the new arrival. Patterns and fabric were carefully selected for the perfect wardrobe. Attention was paid to the smallest detail and every item was tailored to the select doll to assure a perfect fit.

Anticipation found its fulfillment as Autumn squealed with delight that Christmas morning, holding the outfits to her heart and spinning with joy. Her gleeful smile and warm hug were all Carol needed to reward her for the many hours at the fabric shop and sewing machine. But unbeknownst to Autumn, the clothes were not for her present doll, but for a new doll. Unfortunately, the new doll was delayed in shipment and would not arrive for several more days. In the joy of the morning, that vital fact had not been conveyed to the squealing Autumn, who saw the fulfillment of her every dream in the new wardrobe, carefully crafted by hand through love.

Later, when a distraught Autumn bolted from her room, Carol explained to her sobbing grandchild that a new doll was on the way, and she assured her that this doll would fit the clothes. Between sobs and heaves, Autumn began to understand the situation and realized that not only did she have a new set of doll clothes but she was also getting a new doll. In that moment, despair turned to fresh expectation and her festive spirit was restored. As the aroma of roast turkey, fresh baked dinner rolls and pecan pie filled the house, Autumn's sobs gave way to new joy. Such is the easily healed faith of a child.

A few days later, as promised, the precious package arrived and the outfits were a perfect fit. Through the anticipation of a promise, the fulfillment was even greater than the original desire. Both Carol and Autumn experienced the reward only achieved through waiting. Now there were a doll, a new wardrobe that fit it, and two grateful hearts.

I have included this simple story because aspects of Biblical hope closely parallel this Christmas story. The exchange between Autumn and Carol carried an expectation based on the relationship of the giver and the receiver. The gift of a handmade wardrobe held a far greater value than one purchased with a few clicks on Amazon. Carol's investment of time and energy was driven by an anticipation of Autumn's response. The hours of planning, shopping, sewing and wrapping were a strategic venture pregnant with hope for her granddaughter's delight.

Similarly the Spirit of God waits in expectation of our response to His gifts of love. With painstaking care each gift from His heart is carefully designed, knitted together and filled with the Maker's own virtues to fulfill our present and future needs. Near the end of His earthly ministry, Jesus declared over Jerusalem, *"How often I've ached to embrace your children, the way a hen gathers her chicks under her wings,"* (Matt. 23:37 MSG).

God anticipates our reaction to His love much the same way that Carol anticipated Autumn's response to the gift. Similarly, from great tragedy and loss, the Father painstakingly fashioned a fresh future for Cherie. There is no comparison in the life experiences of Autumn and Cherie. My point is the Father's heart toward Cherie was the same as Carol's heart for her granddaughter. He plans, prepares and anticipates our response to His love. This is the nature of eternal, authentic, Biblical hope.

## Intentional Design

God instills in every person a connection to the present and future, to that which is now and that which is coming. Our Creator is the God of the future. Through Him, we know instinctively that we belong in our future, both on earth and beyond. We were breathed into existence with an attachment to the "yet to come." The reality of an eternal future is a natural condition for all human beings.

By design, God has created mankind with a sense of eternity built into our DNA. Like the sweet fragrance of apple blossoms in spring, each life carries the aroma of eternal hope. This eternal part of our makeup gives meaning to our life.

> *He has made everything beautiful in its time. He has also set eternity in the hearts of men; yet they cannot fathom what God has done from beginning to end.*
>
> Ecclesiastes 3:11 (MSG)

Although we live with uncertainty in our daily lives, each of us has an innate, designer-created awareness of eternity—an eternal hope orienting us toward a secure future.

As surely as blossoms yield fruit, so our future is locked in the seed of our hearts, awaiting its time to sprout and grow. Our sense of a secure future is more certain than receiving the perfect Christmas gift from a loving grandmother. As the author of eternity and the designer of mankind, God is our connection with our destiny. Just as He designed the chicks' response to their mother's covering, He put the sense of connection and future into every living thing. All that has life has hope. Then God said,

> *"Let Us make man in Our image, according to Our likeness..."*

> Genesis 1:26 NASB

## Crafted Someones

When God created Adam, He started a line of someones. Every human being is a "someone" born of God. His breath—released into man—continues in the breath of every person. The heartbeat of God echoes in the heartbeat of each one of us. The God of relational hope made us people of relational hope.

We were in God's mind before we were in our mother's womb. *"Before I formed you in the womb I knew you"* (Jeremiah. 1:5 NASB). In some mysterious way, the Creator was thinking about each individual as their spirit of life entered into the womb.

It was God's idea to weave hope and eternity into the fabric of creation. The intentional design of the Father's blueprint for all living things included hope as a foundational element. As His creations, we share in His nature. Our source of life is supplied from One greater than ourselves.

> *For in Him, we live and move and exist, as even some of your own poets have said, "For we also are His children."*

> Acts 17:28 (NASB)

As His offspring, we bear the elements of His nature, the expression of His life.

When God formed Adam, a unique relationship began. With a breath, God started the human family, a line of beings He could befriend and endow. From that beginning, He has formed each person with a unique connection to Him. We learn of this relationship through the deeper understanding of hope that is found in the Bible.

## An Eternity Scripted

On a visit to Sydney Australia, Carol and I, and our son Aaron encountered a unique expression of this sense of future. The word *Eternity* was illuminated in huge neon lights on the Sydney Harbor Bridge. The story goes that a local eccentric, Arthur Stace, travelled the suburbs adorning all the walls he could find with the one word—*Eternity.* In an interview, Stace spoke of his Christian conversion and the ensuing call to adorn the flat spaces of suburbia with his conviction. " *'Eternity' went ringing through my brain and suddenly I began crying and felt a powerful call from the Lord to write 'Eternity.'* " Even though he was illiterate and could hardly write his own name, Arthur said, *"The word 'Eternity' came out smoothly, in a beautiful Copperplate Script. I couldn't understand it, and I still can't."*

Several mornings a week for the next 35 years, Stace left home at 5 a.m. to travel the streets of Sydney and chalk *Eternity* on footpaths, train station entrances, and anywhere inspiration struck. It is estimated that he wrote the word over 500,000 times. Acting anonymously, Stace's identity was finally revealed in a newspaper article in 1956. As a tribute to the man known as

*Mr. Eternity*, the Sydney Harbour Bridge was lit up with the word *Eternity* as part of the celebrations for the 2000 New Year's Eve celebrations as well as the Olympic games.

## Integral Hope

As evidence to the integral nature of hope to our being, most people groups demonstrate a divinely inspired hope with a connection to the future. Researchers have discovered that the roots of eternity cover the earth. Don Richardson, author of various books including *Eternity In Their Hearts*, is a missionary, teacher and international speaker who worked among the tribal people of Western New Guinea, Indonesia. He argues that hidden among tribal cultures are practices or understandings which he calls "redemptive analogies." These can be used to illustrate the meaning of the Christian Gospel, contextualizing the Biblical representation of the incarnation of Jesus. People seem to be instinctively aware of the nature of God and the sense of future, even without being taught. Innate hope is the sense of future built into our very being.

Richardson estimates that about 90% or more of the folk religions on this planet contain clear acknowledgement of the existence of one Supreme God! Further, he details many accounts of the innate characteristic of eternity. He develops the anthropologist's perspective that the nature, role, and characteristics of a sky-god may be called differently but are always recognizable. People groups over the earth know the inner awareness of the eternal Creator's heartbeat. Built in, eternal, authentic hope.

Whether in a granddaughter's Christmas gift, an illiterate's fixation on eternity, or a people group looking for God to fulfill a prophetic tale, hope continues to call mankind toward a promising future. God's covenant with us is assurance that life will have meaning and a future. When God sees a rainbow, He is reminded of His covenant promise and hope toward mankind. To a certain extent, we all *know* that hope and have *eternity in our hearts*.

The focus and proof of our hope is the character and nature of God. The more we know Him, the more settled and powerful our hope becomes. The secure, solid ground from which our hope is expressed is found in the quality of our relationship with God the Hope Giver! This quality of hope can be found in even the youngest of believers.

## Hope In The Room

Brian and Louise Hogan and their four children lived and worked as missionaries among the Mongolian people. The following is Brian's account of his daughter Molly as she reacts to the death of her two-month-old brother Jed (one of the leadership team members, Magnus, was with them):

> While Magnus and I are praying, Molly comes quietly into the room. I stare at her in disbelief at how much grief has changed her. Her eyes are red and puffy, her blond locks tangled and bedraggled, and the tears still flow down her cheeks. She is grieving for her little brother as deeply as any six year old has ever grieved. She hasn't stopped sobbing since I told her the news. I worry that looking at his body, as she is doing, might unhinge her. I can't imagine what this has already done to her young faith and impression of God as her heavenly Father. I ask

her, "Molly, can you still believe that God is good?" And she answers immediately, "Oh yes, Daddy! And He's here in this room with us right now." As she says this, Magnus and I sense the presence of Christ in such a powerful way. Jesus is in the bedroom! Jesus is grieving with us. I have never felt the Lord's presence in that potent form before or since. Even though the miracle we sought doesn't come, we begin to feel hope well up that makes no human sense in our circumstances. (*There's A Sheep In My Bathtub*, www.AsteroideaBooks.com p.160)

Molly's response demonstrates an authentic, life-giving hope from an intimate relationship with Jesus. This degree of authenticity springing from her heart is founded in the simplicity of a child's hope. It is so impactful when our children demonstrate the solid response that we ourselves desire to display. This is what Jesus meant when He said that we must become like little children to receive the kingdom of God. Hope has many dimensions to be considered in developing a holistic definition. Molly's experience illustrates the spiritual dimension, the most accessible aspect to a young child.

All of us need to experience the reality of the simple but powerful spiritual dimension of intimate relationship, just as Molly did. As the fragrance draws one to the bloom, that internal "eternal" is what orients our hope toward a designer-created eternity. Our lives can demonstrate the settled, focused hope connected to the nature and character of God. There is an intentional design of future in all DNA. We will now look deeper into the nature of authentic hope.

## Summary

Some of the ideas we have considered in understanding hope:

- We are designed with a sense of future and an eternal hope.
- Relational hope is God's idea and pattern.
- Hope is instinctive and eternal throughout all creation.
- A sense of eternity keeps us connected to the future.
- The focus of Biblical hope is the character and nature of God.

Here are some scriptures considered in this chapter:

Jeremiah 1:5, 31:17 NIV; Proverbs 11:7, 23:17-18 NIV; Psalms. 22:9 AMP, 62:5, 71:5 NIV; Job 11:18 NIV; Matthew 23:37 MSG; Acts: 17:28 NASB; Genesis 1:26, 9:15 NASB; Ecclesiastes. 3:11 NIV, MSG.

**LET'S CONNECT TO DISCUSS THIS CHAPTER:**

**Join My Interactive Discussions:** Please come visit with me at www.IncreaseHope.com in section "Book Resources" where I will be posting specifically for this chapter. I invite you to leave your comments or questions and I'll personally be responding. I will also have audios and videos and other resources pertinent to the topics in this chapter.

**Join Our Live Events:** Carol and I also offer special events www.HopeAcceleratorSeminars.com for more personal and in-depth face to face training and equipping. I look forward to continued connection with you.

Blessings! - Arnold J. Allen

## *Personal Notes*

_____

_____

_____

_____

_____

_____

_____

_____

_____

_____

_____

_____

_____

_____

_____

_____

_____

_____

_____

_____

_____

_____

_____

_____

_____

_____

_____

_____

*"We know in our bones that hope is everything. In the back of our minds, we suspect that it is nothing at all."*

(Maurice Lamm, *The Power of Hope*, p.15)

*Return to our fortress, O prisoners who have the hope.*

Zechariah 9:12

# 2
# The Marrow of Hope

## A Source of Life in our Bones

The tension between our heart and mind is felt acutely when we are trying to understand authentic hope. This is because the "in our bones" that Maurice Lamm, author of *The Power of Hope,* speaks of is a real dimension of our makeup. Yet for many of us the suspicion of our mind tends to undo the powerful effects of hope. Most of us are mentored more in suspicious doubt than in anticipatory, authentic hope, making our grasp of that hope tenuous at best.

Developing a definition of hope must include the thinking, as well as the emotional, processes of our inner world. Dr. Groopman describes his journey in his book *Anatomy of Hope.*

> Hope is one of our central emotions, but we are often at a loss when asked to define it. Many of us confuse hope with optimism, a prevailing attitude that "things will turn out for the best." But hope differs from optimism. Hope does not arise from being told

to "think positively" or from hearing an overly rosy forecast. Hope, unlike optimism, is rooted in unalloyed (pure) reality. Hope is the elevating feeling we experience when we see—in the mind's eye—a path to a better future. Hope acknowledges the significant obstacles and deep pitfalls along the path. True hope has no room for delusion. Clear-eyed, hope gives us the courage to confront our circumstances and the capacity to surmount them.

In addition to thoughts and emotions, hope carries an inner understanding. It is "in our bones" as Lamm tells us in the quote above. Hope is an innate ability to realize the sense, the power and the purpose of life. It is more than developing a positive prognosis and striving for it to come to pass. The prognosis may be a complete fog. While expressing hope often includes imagining a positive outcome, it is more than creative imagination—more than developing something in which to believe. Yes, hope is tied to what we believe, but it refuses to be confined to a belief system. Hope is the nature of life, the nature of authentic relationship.

## Defining the indefinable

One of our greatest challenges in forming a working definition of authentic, Biblical hope is that hope is cloaked in mystery. Still, by reaching into the unseen world of hope, we can identify its salient qualities. An important aspect of hope is that it is focused on an eternal track record—that which already exists! Rather than focus on what may or may not come into our lives, hope is consumed with the One who is already in our lives. The nature and character of God—His faithfulness, love, kindness, resourcefulness, goodness—is the central focus of Biblical hope. Since authentic hope is sourced in relationship, and because all life comes from the same source, each of us is infused with hope. It really is "in our bones."

Authentic, Biblical hope finds its orientation in a primary, significant relationship. The sweet fragrance of the apple blossom, the tender connection of Molly Hogan, and the personal investment of a grandmother into a special Christmas gift are each sourced by the same life-giving relationship. This creates an expectation oriented toward the future. The nature of this hope is an expectation that God will relate to us in the future just as He has been relating to people for generations. Certainly, there is confusion within us in some areas where we have concluded that God has not treated us well or that things have turned out poorly due to God's negligence. However, the confusion is between the truth of Who He is and our contaminated thinking.

We actually have a history of God relating to us even if we are unaware of it. We can learn this history from Scripture, discovering how Jesus thinks about us. He tends to always act with certain qualities or characteristics toward us. Of course, this is similar to all of our relationship. We expect that our family members and friends will continue to relate to us pretty much the same way that they have for years. And while even the most stalwart person is fickle when compared to God, the principle is the same. What God always brings to the table is the same amazing Guy! The idea that God will always act in a loving way toward us is a very hope-filled idea.

Hope makes sense by its nature. It is not the same as being happy that things are going well. Often, things are not going well at all. Yet, hope knows "in the bones" that all things make sense and have value, regardless of how they turn out. This universal quality of hope vastly improves the quality of our life experience. For a low-hope person, the job lay-off notice might ignite curses for his boss, his wife, the dog, the president, God and anyone else who comes to mind. In contrast, the high-hope response doesn't deny the difficulty, but experiences an overriding assurance of God's peace while anticipating what God has next. Hope anticipates God showing up in the emerging future.

So hope possesses an intuitive element, that gut feeling, as well as an intellectual understanding. The intuitive energy, the emotion and the intelligence of potential are required for a complete definition of hope. In a creative, forward-moving operation, hope musters the resources of spirit, soul, mind and body to harness sustaining energy. Authentic hope engages that which is locked up "in the bones" as well as creative hypostasizing. Dr. Groopman quotes Dr. Davidson this way:

> What I would call affective forecasting—that is, the comforting, energizing, elevating feeling that you experience when you project in your mind a positive future. This requires the brain to generate a different affective, or feeling, state than the one you are currently in.

## The Source

In addition to this, hope draws upon a supporting relationship and projects a positive, life-giving energy into the future. This supportive power and sustaining energy do more than affect how we respond to situations; they actually influence how things unfold. This is because Biblical hope assumes God and His Word as the source of hopeful energy and ideas. He is the source of the force of life as well as the source of creative ideas that become expressed in life. Therefore, our limited creative abilities are expanded as we partner with the divine source of creative thinking—God himself.

Christ is not simply the ground upon Whom the hope rests. Rather, He is the sphere and element in Whom the hope is placed. Hope is a relationship with a living person. Scripture describes having hope in Christ.

> *In his great mercy he has given us new birth into a living hope through the resurrection of Jesus Christ from the dead,*
>
> I Peter 1:3 (NIV)

> *To them God has chosen to make known among the Gentiles the glorious riches of this mystery, which is Christ in you, the hope of glory.*

Colossians 1:27 (NIV)

> *He is not far from each one of us. "For in him we live and move and have our being."*
>
> Acts 17:27-28a (NIV)

Hope is connected not only to events, mental images,

expectations and ideas, but more importantly to a person. This is a fundamental truth that radically alters how we experience life. Authentic hope—the real deal—must be understood in relation to a person or group of people. Far from a nebulous concept or idea, authentic Biblical hope is about real people in real relationship with a real God. This sense of eternity, the energy of expectation and anticipation of favor, finds its expression in relationship.

The Biblical definition of hope includes expectation, confidence and favor. The expectation of authentic hope is an anticipation of success and fulfillment. It is an expectation that desires the future. It is an expectation of relationship. It is an eager looking forward toward experiencing the fruit of relationship, much the way that Carol looked forward to Autumn's joy-filled response in Chapter 1.

## Expectation of Promise

The depth of anticipation that characterizes hope results from head and heart connected in life experience. As we think and feel the expectation of a promising future, the focus becomes relationship. Authentic hope is a passion that my relationship with God will result in a good outcome. It is a passion that skews my thoughts and heart toward expecting that His goodness and kindness will show up. I think and act as though God is designing a great future for me because He is! Much like a first love experience, our heart, thoughts, and emotions are consumed with expectation of Him.

The nature of hope includes an eagerness to experience God's presence, provision and promises in our future. This is not a focus on getting stuff. Instead, it is a focus on the relationship involved. For Carol, the doll clothes for Autumn carried an anticipation of response. For Autumn, part of the joyous anticipation of the new wardrobe was knowing how happy it would make Grandma to see her enjoying the clothes. The energy and power of emotion, both pain and joy, created a deeper, fuller relationship experience. Authentic hope is about an ever-deepening relationship. It is God's anticipation of our response as well as our anticipation of giving Him joy! It carries an expectation of Him coming into our life situations.

## The Confidence of Hope

Hope is assurance in Someone. Inherent in this assurance is the ability of this Someone to act in a proper, trustworthy, and reliable manner. When we have hope, we know that this Someone is going to consistently act in such a way that we can fully, confidently trust ourselves to Him and know that He is trusting us. *Trust in the Lord and do good; dwell in the land and enjoy safe pasture* (Psalms 37:3 NIV).

Our confidence is that God will act with love, kindness and goodness toward us. In turn, His confidence is that we will respond to Him in love, honor and respect. This mutual confidence is based on the character of those in the relationship—His perfect character and our redeemed character.

Our anticipation in God is distinguished by confidence rather than anxiety. Biblical hope carries an expectation that completely lacks doubt about God's character, power, motives and ways. *Everyone who has this hope in him purifies himself, just as he is pure* (I John 3:3 NIV).

This type of hope is illustrated in the story of the three Hebrew servants: Shadrach, Meshach and Abednego, from Daniel Chapter 3. They defied King Nebuchadnezzar by refusing to worship an idol. At the pivotal point in the story, they expressed the type of confidence provided by Biblical hope.

> *Shadrach, Meshach, and Abednego answered King Nebuchadnezzar, "Your threats mean nothing to us. If you throw us in the fire, the God we serve can rescue us from your roaring furnace and anything else you might cook up, O king. But even if he doesn't, it won't make a bit of difference, O king. We still wouldn't serve your gods or worship the gold statue you set up."*

Daniel 3:16-18 (MGS)

They expressed confidence in God's care for them. They did not know what God was going to do but they trusted Him. The phrase, "But even if he doesn't," was not expressed in doubt. Rather, authentic, Biblical hope simply does not know what the outcome will be. It does not know what will happen or why situations transpire the way that they do. It only knows Who is handling the process. It knows Who will be the same at the end of the day. The outcome is a characteristic of the relationship. Confidence in God's trustworthiness is held without question until no other questions matter.

## Personal Definition

We sometimes need to listen to our own conversation to discover our personal definition of hope. A few years ago, I worked as a carpenter to pay my way through graduate school. A friend, Daniel, needed a deck built around his swimming pool. As with most of the work I did for him over the years, he did not give me much detail. "Make it from about here to there. Use your judgment on the rest of it. I have confidence in you." He had confidence in my ability to do a good job and satisfy the need within a reasonable price. This confidence was based on both my track record with past jobs and our personal relationship.

While Daniel expressed his confidence as: "I know who you are, what you can do and how you have treated me in the past," he could just as well have expressed his confidence in Biblical language by saying: "I hope that you do a good and reasonable job." With a Biblical understanding of hope, the meaning would have been the same. Of course, if he had said that in the common understanding of hope, I would have had a very different sense of his confidence in my abilities. However, Biblical hope is able to say: "I hope God will treat me kindly" and mean: "I am confident that God will deal kindly and justly with me while showing His goodness to me."

The Biblical definition of hope carries this sense of deep confidence. It has an unshakable assurance in the goodness of God and His intention to deal with us in a favorable way.

> *I will look to the Lord and confident in Him I will keep watch; I will wait with hope and expectancy for the God of my salvation; my God will hear me.*

> Micah 7:7 AMP

Authentic hope is a confidence in the favor of God regardless of the outcome.

## The Spirit of Favor

> *Set your hope wholly and unchangeably on the grace (divine favor) that is coming to you….*

> I Peter 1:13 (AMP)

In addition to confidence and assurance, Biblical hope involves favor. Favor is an act of kindness performed out of good will with an approving, friendly or supportive attitude. Hope carries an instinctive understanding of favorable treatment by God and others; we know God's favor.

> *Yet the Lord longs to be gracious to you; he rises to show you compassion. For the Lord is a God of justice. Blessed are all who wait for him!*

> Isaiah 30:18 (NIV)

This preferential treatment of the one who hopes gives advantage in life and relationship.

Most of us know times when we have experienced favor times when there was a visible force working in our advantage. Yet the spirit of favor, as some have described this force, has power to significantly alter situations. It is as though an energy is at work that draws preference. Similar to a magnet on metal, the power of favor pulls help, support and cooperation into situations. God calls us to hope, and inherent in that call is His intention to act with favor toward us and energize others to demonstrate favor in our direction.

It has been a great joy to have grandchildren, to be with them and play simple games with the young ones. One of those games is drawing with metal grindings in a plastic case. It is really an art. The goal is to take a magnetic pencil, place it under the container and pull the metal grindings into a shape or picture. Viewed from the top, the pencil is unseen, but the results are observed as the black metal is pulled into place. This is how favor works on our behalf. The unseen power of favor pulls situations into place. The force of favor works to our benefit.

In the ancient story, Shadrach, Meshach, and Abednego experienced the favor of King Nebuchadnezzar. He gave them positions of influence. But in an even greater way, they experienced the favor of God giving them even more influential positions right in the fiery furnace. God's presence joined them in the midst of their trial. Biblical hope is favor. God's presence joins us in the furnace of life just as Brian Hogan and his daughter Molly experienced in those hours after losing little Jed.

As a young pastor in the early '70s, I was treated with a favor that sometimes embarrassed me. One day I went to the local city office to pay a parking ticket. Noticing the "Reverend" title on my driver's license, the clerk said, "There is no fine for you." From the surprised look on my face the clerk surmised that this was my first trip to her office. So she explained that the city recognized the important role of the clergy and understood that situations arise that result in expired parking meters. As a favor to the clergy there were no parking fines. She explained that any future tickets simply needed to be noted with "clergy" and dropped in the mail. This was a favor to the office or position of clergyman.

Favor was extended to me in other ways as well. As I visited various homes of the congregation, the finest baked goods and tea were served on fine china. Although the people of the Atlantic Canada region where I served were very hospitable by nature, I experienced special favor as a pastor. They were honored that I would visit their homes, listen to their needs and pray with them. I experienced their favor as I served them. It was a humbling experience. Favor grew as I buried their loved ones, performed marriages and dedicated their young children. The best part however, was seeing that favor move from honor toward the pastoral office to a heart response to me as I cared for them. Favor became a part of the relationship. While I gave honor and favor to the people I served, they responded in honor and favor toward me.

This is the transition that God intends for our relationship with Him. As we express honor and favor toward Him, honor and favor are released from Him toward us.

> *For the eyes of the Lord run to and fro throughout the whole earth, to show Himself strong on behalf of those whose heart is loyal to Him*

> II Chronicles 16:9 (NKJV)

It is not about performing to get another person to act in a certain way. A posture such as this would be considered control or performance-oriented behavior. Rather, it means that mature relationships are characterized by loyalty, honor and favor flowing in both directions. The three Hebrew men favored God over the king. This act resulted in one of the most amazing miracles ever recorded. They were completely untouched by the flames that killed the soldiers throwing them into the furnace. That great favor was compounded by an extremely rare event. God showed up as a man walking with them in the flames. They honored and favored God, in return, He honored and favored them. The fruit of increased quality of relationship is increased favor. Similar to the magnetic art game that I played with my grandchildren, we hold the magnetic stick creating favor that honors God. At the same time, He uses favor and honor creating His own art work in our lives.

It is God's intention that hope be part of a whole life experience. He has placed expectation within us, deep in our bones. By design, we expect Him to show Himself to us. Confidence is a characteristic of a solid relationship. Confidence and favor are certain experience when we know authentic hope.

## Summary

Some of the ideas we have considered in understanding hope:

- Hope includes mind, heart, intuition.
- Authentic hope is sourced in relationship.
- Authentic hope is a relational passion.
- Hope does not know the outcome of situations.
- Hope is characterized by confidence and favor.

Some scriptures considered in this chapter:

> I Peter 1:3, 1:13; Psalms 37:3; I John 3:3; Daniel 3:16-18; Micah 7:7; Isaiah 30:18; II Chronicles 16:9

## LET'S CONNECT TO DISCUSS THIS CHAPTER:

**Join My Interactive Discussions:** Please come visit with me at www.IncreaseHope.com in section "Book Resources" where I will be posting specifically for this chapter. I invite you to leave your comments or questions and I'll personally be responding. I will also have audios and videos and other resources pertinent to the topics in this chapter.

**Join Our Live Events:** Carol and I also offer special events www.HopeAcceleratorSeminars.com for more personal and in-depth face to face training and equipping. I look forward to continued connection with you.

Blessings! - Arnold J. Allen

**Personal Notes**

_____
_____
_____
_____
_____
_____
_____
_____
_____
_____
_____
_____
_____
_____
_____
_____
_____
_____
_____
_____
_____
_____
_____
_____
_____

The inclusive, relational posture that God assumes toward us produces a sense of transcendence.

*Against all hope, Abraham, in hope believed..."*

Romans 4:18 (NIV)

# 3
# Transcendent Hope

## Connected beyond natural limits

Transcendence is the capacity of hope to make connections that are not experienced through other means. It is characterized by the ability to rise above difficulties and engage with a much larger way of experiencing life. Words like: exceed, unlimited, unconfined, unmatched, and mystical define transcendence. Generally, these words and concepts are not part of our daily thinking, dialogue, or common usage.

Innate is defined as integral, built-in, a natural unlearned aspect of our nature. To have hope at the moment of conception is as natural as the heart to beat at 18 days. This chapter will include the relationship of transcendence and innate aspects of hope.

A friend, Krys, described the experience of her needy friend. Kathy had been severely injured and was in a coma. Because she had been on life support for an extended period and showed no response to human activity or medication, they were considering removal of the life support equipment. The weight of the situation was overwhelming.

Because there were no brain wave activities Kathy's condition seemed beyond hope and carried a high possibility of severe brain damage even if she did emerge from her coma. Praying for God's intervention however, her husband Dave wasn't ready to give up. Knowing that people sometimes respond to the presence of their pet, Dave brought Kathy's dog to the hospital for a visit. Miraculously the dog connected with something in Kathy that sparked a change of direction. Brain waves were detected and she started to respond. Over many days she gradually improved and was eventually released from hospital. Although Kathy still had a long journey of recovery, the power of hope transcended the natural realm and created a response that resulted in life becoming restored. Other than problems with short term memory, Kathy is alive and thriving nearly 15 years later. Hope prevailed. Transcendent hope became manifest.

While transcendence is an important aspect of hope, it is also an important part of relationship experiences and core beliefs. Authentic hope is not only present in the world that we know, but is also rooted in mystery. The transcendent dimension is "other worldly": a dimension beyond the natural, material world. I am not referring to something spooky. I am simply identifying an aspect of one's experience is an unseen, larger dimension of existence.

Our core beliefs are the foundation of how we live and conduct relationship. These are learned, developed, and guided by both past experiences and beliefs about the future. To transcend these beliefs is to make room for the mystery of hope. When we are convinced that there is a reality that is not limited to our past experiences or future belief, we want to engage that reality. This is what Romans 4:18 is speaking about. It could well be translated: *Alongside the hope that he already had experienced and was walking in, Abraham was convinced that a much greater, transcendent hope could be trusted.* The Greek word translated "against" is *para*, commonly used as "alongside" or "in conjunction with." With transcendence as part of his core belief Abraham was able to engage a transcendent dimension of hope alongside his innate hope.

Just as Abraham did, we can also discover an increased activity of hope in this larger, transcendent realm. Heart connection in worship or prayer is transcendence. The sense of being part of a much larger scheme of things or discovering spiritual revelation are elements of transcendent activity. We connect with a much larger, fuller experience of life, love and personhood beyond our realm of resource and reference. To experience authentic hope involves a larger, transcendent experience.

We might say, *"Alongside all hope, Thomas Edison or Nelson Mandela or Mother Theresa or Steve Jobs, in hope believed."* Anyone, including you and me, who has reached beyond their possible and into the impossible could put their name in here. I am not suggesting that anyone in history could possibly match Abraham, the Father of Faith! However, I do want to point out the relationship of different dimensions of hope. As we believe there is something or someone to reach for just beyond the horizon, we reach for it. We hope alongside all hope! We "para" or join our hope with transcendence. Or more accurately, transcendence becomes manifest in our experience.

Transcendent hope finds us. Our hope is inspired by a sense of promise—energized by a greater power sustained in the struggle—through connectedness to the greater as it reaches for the impossible.

## But Hope Anyway

Less esoteric than Edison or Jobs, my mom in hope believed in my abusive, alcoholic father when there was little evidence in his behavior to support belief or hope. When he took the evening meal from the stove and fed it to the dogs, she hoped alongside hope. When she expected a kiss and he instead bit her lips until they bled, she hoped alongside hope. When farm tools and equipment were pawned to buy brandy, she hoped alongside hope. When the family farm was signed away for debt, she hoped alongside hope. For six weeks of his life-or-death stay in ICU, she hoped alongside hope. When he recovered, dry from booze, free from the death grip, she said, "I have the man that I married back again." Transcendent hope sustained innate hope for the fruit of endurance.

There were many very difficult times and seasons in her journey. Many times she felt like there was no future. Often feeling trapped and unable to escape the pain, she knew she had to go another day. With responsibility for the farm and 10 children, she needed strength. The life-sustaining energy of transcendent hope kept her another day. Through the support of family, friends, and the Spirit of life, she was sustained. Her decades of innate hope alongside transcendent hope paid off in this life in four final years together. And now, with Dad's renewed relationship with Jesus, they enjoy eternity together.

The inclusive, relational posture that God assumes toward us produces a sense of transcendence. Authentic transcendent hope joins innate hope to create expectation of a good outcome beyond our natural understanding and limited emotional and material resources.

Transcendence enables innate hope to fulfill its design. As with Abraham, each individual destiny is influenced by hope. The partnership of Divine, transcendent hope and innate hope is the expression of the Hebrew words for hope, *"tiqwah"* and *"ahriyt,"* as described in Appendix A. Psalms 22:9 in the Amplified Bible brings these two together: "You made me hope and trust when I was on my mother's breast." Divine, transcendent hope energy flows into innate hope and empowering the unfolding destiny of each person.

## Hope In Genes

I often think of this connection in the unfolding mystery of metamorphosis. The fascinating journey of caterpillar to butterfly provides an illustration of the transcendent and innate partnership. Indeed, He designed transcendence in DNA. The insect's DNA receives divine energy in its unfolding journey. The transcendent activity of DNA is observed in the incredible life span of the salmon. Hatching from eggs in the creek bed, growing to adulthood in the stream, swimming for some of years in the ocean and at times returning to the exact beginning of the journey to spawn the next generation, expresses a divine code. Similarly, the destiny of each human DNA is designed to access the divine in its unfolding journey. Obviously, human DNA is not as simple as an insect or fish, yet the principle is the same. The power of transcendent hope partners with innate hope in creating design, finding expression and fulfilling destiny.

Research on human DNA confirms the transcendent power of innate hope. DNA from donors was placed in special containers, allowing trained observers to record changes. As emotional stimulation was given to the donor, the DNA in the containers exhibited emotional peaks and valleys that matched the donor. Although the containers of DNA were moved up to 350 miles away, there was no lag time, no transmission time. The researchers concluded that a previously unrecognized form of non-local energy allows transcendent communication. Other DNA research illustrates the powerful, positive effect of transcendent activities such as meditation, prayer, and worship. Positive emotions such as hope demonstrate good results in mental, physical and spiritual wellness. I will describe this more in later chapters. My point here is simply: transcendent activity exists and we respond to transcendence mentally, physically, and spiritually. Authentic, transcendent hope therefore is an essential to every successful outcome of human endeavor.

## Secure Attachment

Authentic hope develops in trusting relationships during life's formative years. God intended that we be nurtured in hope so that we can nurture others into a hope-filled posture. Secure attachments to a caregiver provide children with a model for effective, goal-related activities and experiences of hope. Loving attachment provides an environment where children learn to think of themselves as successful, both now and in the future. Interpersonal relationships are primary to the development of hope in the formative years and throughout life. In the midst of this environment, the Spirit of God is active in the healthy development of hope. One might imagine the Spirit singing over the womb as we each are conceived and become a living soul. This personal, individual love song is never interrupted nor ever ends throughout life. An aspect of transcendent hope is the perpetual flow of divine energy into each individual. Unfortunately, enemies are also at work in resisting the development and renewal of hope and must be dealt with. Even within trusting relationships, hope does not grow unopposed. Developing and maintaining trust is vital for hope-filled relationships and life experience.

## Heart and Head

Life consists both of things learned and things experienced. Clearly we learn through the intellect as well as the heart. But there are certain aspects of learning that do not fit either category. These come to us as transcendent experience, like the change of season when the smell of spring is in the air. At times, hope emerges as subtly as summer yields to fall. At this moment I am experiencing the warmth of wood burning in the fireplace in my living room. Although I may be able to help you intellectually understand the feeling of the warm fire on a cold spring day in the Washington Mountains, you need to experience it to really connect with what I am describing. We learn and experience hope in heart, mind and beyond.

We experience people and we experience life. Sometimes the experience is good, other times not so good. So it goes.

Authentic hope requires a relational experience demonstrating hope. According to the original design, the authentic experience of hope that began in heaven is to continue in the womb. A hope atmosphere, in the womb and beyond, fosters knowledge springing from the heart-connection with the Giver of life and one's parents. Authentic hope imparts a living energy—an inner knowing—every person is designed to experience throughout all of life.

In our relational experience with God, He intends all of our experiences of Him be good ones, leading us into His goodness. The more we experience God, the greater our opportunity to experience authentic hope. Some people know about God. Others have followed His laws most of their lives. Many others have been part of a religious experience at some time. However, that is not the same as experiencing Him. Experiencing the fullness of authentic hope involves experiencing God's goodness in a deep, personal way at the core of one's being.

## Core Beliefs: Stamped and Developing

A core belief creates a settled persuasion combining head knowledge and heart values together into a firm confidence. By design, fundamental core beliefs were imprinted into human DNA at conception. Hope is one of those core beliefs in the body, soul and spirit of every human being, indeed in every living thing. The expectation of a good future, and being part of that future, is fundamental to human makeup. Access to the transcendent hope dimension is also fundamental for everyone. As life unfolds from conception, each individual develops beliefs from l fe situations. Each belief is unique to each individual. At times it is positive, other times it is negative. The knowledge and values that we have naturally at birth are nurtured by good and bad experiences. Innate core beliefs develop into settled persuasions for each individual.

The f re in the kiln of life experience tests the essence of developing persuasions—one's core beliefs. Life's trials and tests help establish core beliefs. Response in life experiences decides whether we hang on to a core belief, adjust it, or let it go. Rarely do we ever really think about our core beliefs, yet we live by them every day. All of our important choices and attitudes are an expression of these settled persuasions. All relaticnships and acquired goals are a demonstration of beliefs. Hope-filled people carry expressions of hope into relationships and goals. Through the kiln of life experience, innate hope influences core beliefs.

Core beliefs based on experience have a foundation of truth or myth, healthy or toxic. Myths are real beliefs based on mistaken ideas. Myths are always toxic in relationship. The negative power of toxic beliefs manifests in physical, emotional, and spiritual illness. Healthy, positive, truth-based beliefs create and energize wellness, wholeness, and connectedness. Many beliefs are a mix of truth and fiction thus, to some degree, we live with a tension. Innate hope pulls the heart and mind toward a promising future, expecting a good outcome. Fear, pain and disappointment from life experiences try to shut hope down, or at least hinder its positive effectiveness. These negative forces resist authentic hope while truth strengthens hope-filled experience. Relationships are the fruit of core beliefs and will depend upon the quality of foundation they are built upon.

We all have core beliefs in every relationship area. Friendship, romance, marriage, communication, parenting, finances, spirituality and work ethic are some of the many areas based on core beliefs. Our persuasions influencing hope in these areas are a fundamental part of how we live life. Identifying and working with our core belief of authentic hope is essential. It is vital to affirm true persuasions regarding hope and eliminate identified toxic myths. Myths resist the positive effects of one's original, hope-oriented design. Truth must replace myth. Adjusting beliefs requires embracing perpetual change. Authentic hope provides energy to essential, positive, life-giving change. True or mythical core beliefs, coupled with emotional and spiritual energy, are demonstrated in relationship.

## From The Heart

Sometimes there is a deep wondering in the most personal areas of the heart—a yearning or longing for life situations to make sense. It's too deep for words but craves expression, so our thoughts race:

> *"Why is this happening to me?"*
> *"What did I do to deserve this type of treatment?"*
> *"If I had been there, would it have happened?"*
> *"Why is it always my fault?"*
> *"It's not right! Why did this happen?"*

Hopelessly struggling with these heart-wrenching questions doesn't bring any peace; it only makes us feel worse and leads us to destructive conclusions:

*"Maybe life wouldn't be so hard if I wasn't so stupid."*

*"If I wasn't around, this stuff wouldn't happen."*

*"Everything would work better if somebody else did it!"*

While we are wise not to act on these conclusions, nothing gets resolved without hope. Eventually the negative monologue gets tucked away somewhere. I'm not sure where it goes, but life goes on as we put one foot in front of the other. It is not just a choice to move on. It is energy joined with choice that moves us forward. Sometimes that energy is just there and emerges like helium filling a balloon. At other times, the companionship of a friend adds energy like pumping air into a deflated bike tire. Occasionally, we are so flat that intervening energy feels like connecting booster cables to a dead car battery or an I.V. bottle to a vein. This was Kathy's state when she lay in the hospital bed without brain waves. When we are this low, it seems like the power to go forward has to come from somewhere outside of ourselves. And indeed, through transcendent hope, power comes.

This energy is a living power—the power of hope, the energy of life. By intentional design, God has placed in every living thing an ability to access an unlimited energy empowering the ability to rise above the present difficulties. It is a life-sustaining force that is not easily recognized in the midst of our trials. Often we only recognize the fruit of transcendent hope as we reflect on our past experiences. We have all made or heard comments describing transcendence.

*"I don't know how I made it through."*

*"It seemed like I was being carried!"*

*"I didn't think that I could survive one more day."*
*The power of living hope sustains life.*

## Knowing—The Eyes of the Heart

There is a particular aspect of core beliefs and persuasion described as "knowing." The relationship of knowing and hope is evident in the Scripture.

The Apostle Paul puts it this way:

> *I pray also that the eyes of your heart may be enlightened in order that you may know the hope to which he has called you, the riches of his glorious inheritance in the saints, and his incomparably great power for us who believe.*

> Ephesians 1:18-19 (NIV)

The Message Bible puts it this way.

> *I ask—ask the God of our Master, Jesus Christ, the God of glory -- to make you intelligent and discerning in knowing him personally, your eyes focused and clear so that you can see exactly what it is he is calling you to do, grasp the immensity of this glorious way of life he has for Christians.*

In order for God's change in our lives to be lasting and effective, we must be able to change our core beliefs. A persuasion toward a new direction becomes established as our hope energizes our beliefs and empowers our choices. Hope has real power when it is characterized by the intelligent, transcendent, discerning "knowing" that Paul describes above.

We all deal with difficulties and tragedies, successes and victories. Our ability to navigate the resulting outcome is according to the maturity of our character and personality.

> *We continue to shout our praise even when we are hemmed in with trouble, because we know how troubles can develop passionate patience in us.*
>
> Romans 5:3 (MSG)

If we are hope-filled people, our response to life situations demonstrates it. Hopelessness, despair and apathy generate different results. A hopeful response born of persuasion, known in the heart and mind, increases both success and enjoyment of life in all circumstances. This is authentic hope.

## Amiee

During her senior year in high school, our daughter Amiee became ill. One day, while walking home from class, she just wanted to lie down on the street to sleep. Through the following days, the fatigue did not pass. She became weaker as we desperately sought to find cause. Days turned into weeks and months as we sought medical treatment and gathered prayer support for God's intervention. Eventually, the diagnosis of chronic fatigue syndrome (CFS), a relatively new disease at the time, put a label on her symptoms. It provided some definition but gave few answers as to what to expect or where we might go for help.

One evening after dinner I found her on her knees at the

bathroom sink as she brushed her teeth. She didn't have the strength to stand. I carried her to bed that night, physically and in my heart. The questions continued. Is this a spiritual issue? Had the doctors missed something? Was there really such an illness as CFS? Why was there no treatment? What about school? What would her young life come to? Our hope clung only to knowing that God was good, full of compassion and desired her best. She had a "future and a hope" in Him (Proverbs 23:18 NIV). Life became a process of renewing our hope in Him while little or no hope existed in the natural.

One morning, sitting in another doctor's office, she began to gently weep. Months of pain and frustration had finally found some connection. The doctor had just finished telling his story of recovery from CFS. Hope began to increase. Relief came just from knowing that someone understood her and how she felt. Maybe these symptoms were for real and not just in her head as some had suggested. Maybe they could be overcome. This was a turning point for her and our family. The hope that we had known in our hearts—hope that had sustained us over the months—was now joined with the possibility of relief— maybe even recovery.

This *knowing* persuasion, an inner understanding, is a deep settled presupposition forming the foundation for life choices and relationship. It is a foundation formed from the revelation that God is good, He is love and every act and motive of His is for my best. God is for me and happy to be that way. The foundation of the future is a settled, *known* persuasion.

## Revelation—The Source

Hope operates in the unseen and the future, that which we cannot see with eyes but perceive from the heart.

> *For in this hope we were saved. But hope that is seen is no hope at all. Who hopes for what he already has? But if we hope for what we do not yet have, we wait for it patiently.*

> Romans 8:24-25 (NIV)

Like hope, the promises of God are based on what we do not yet have, what we do not see. I converse often with people who are experiencing deep disappointment over unfulfilled promises of God. At times, the disappointment is beating them up. Rather than being able to put the promises into the "yet to be fulfilled" category, they label them as "God did not come through." When I can help them see that hope deferred is not hope denied, they start to make real progress in their lives. God's promises are yet to be fulfilled.

This yearning for fulfillment illustrates that hope is innate to our beings.

> *Anyone who is among the living has hope – even a live dog is better off than a dead lion.*

> Ecclesiastes 9:4 (NIV)

When God breathed each of us into the womb, an element of hope came with His breath. This rudimentary seed of hope is part of life, a part of who we are as human beings. And although we have it within us, the development and maturing of hope takes place through the process of revelation. Revelation is a central key to understanding spiritual truth. We come to know God because He reveals himself to us. The fullness of innate, authentic hope is acquired by revelation.

Jesus came to reveal the Father. The Spirit always remains with us to make the person of Jesus and His will known in us. While some aspects of hope can be learned or perceived, the fullness of hope is revealed. It is disclosed by the Spirit to our spirit. Jesus talked about knowing the Father. Because we know Jesus, we can come to know the Father. Because Biblical hope is based on relationship, it is necessary to come to know Jesus in a personal way in order to develop the fullness of authentic hope. It is in the context of that personal relationship that hope has the possibility of becoming known in its deepest form. To know the Father is to know the source of authentic hope.

## Open Eyes by Revelation

Early in our spiritual journey as a couple, Carol and I began to desire a deeper understanding and experience in the things of the Spirit. Although I was a Bible school graduate and pastor, certain gifts and manifestations of the Holy Spirit were considered not to be for today's experience by our denomination. At one point in our pursuit of insight and truth, God began to reveal a new understanding to us. The Scriptures that we had used to argue against the things of the Spirit began to say something quite different to us. Interestingly, this revelation came directly to us. Although we were influenced by other believers, we were not being taught by a bible teacher of a different persuasion. We were not reading books that tried to convince us differently. The only explanation of our change of perspective was the revealing activity of the Spirit of God. Not only did we experience a change in perspective, but our lives were radically changed. We began to live what had been revealed to us. This transition was due to revelation in our hearts.

A few years later, a similar revealing began to take place for me in my understanding of hope. We were leading a discipleship school in Youth With A Mission in the late '70s. Jim Dawson, the international pastor for YWAM at the time, spoke in our school. As Jim and I discussed faith, I found myself distinguishing between hope and faith. He was impressed and challenged me to pursue a study of hope. As with all deep spiritual truth, insight is more about the revealing than the learning. I am now sharing that revealing journey with you, my readers.

Hope has the power to change our lives. Learning about hope, dealing with deferred hope and practicing hopeful responses results in a greater enjoyment of life. Learning hope is significant, but the revelation of hope to the heart by the Spirit alters who we are—just as I was changed by revelation. Revelation does not merely add to head knowledge. Instead, revelation alters who we are.

> But as it is written: "Eye has not seen, nor ear heard, Nor have entered into the heart of man the things which God has prepared for those who love Him." But God has revealed them to us through His Spirit. For the Spirit searches all things, yes, the deep things of God. For what man knows the things of a man except the spirit of the man which

*is in him? Even so no one knows the things of God except the Spirit of God. Now we have received, not the spirit of the world, but the Spirit who is from God, that we might know the things that have been freely given to us by God.*

I Corinthians 2:9-12 (NJKV)

New insight from revelation knowledge reforms our beings like a potter's fingers on clay. I am changed because of the revealing of hope. I become more confident in God's passion to care for me. I expect His favor. I expect Him to show up in the circumstances of life. I anticipate His love. I feel like I have been on the potter's wheel.

Revelation is a bit like falling in love. It changes the chemistry of the relationship. We begin to see and experience things differently. A change takes place as we become significantly connected with another. Similarly, hope, faith and love are revealed in ways that significantly connect us with God. This kind of revealed heart connection fundamentally changes us. We continue to fall in love with who we discover God to be.

Revelation of the person of Jesus Christ is essential to understanding the full spectrum of hope. A deeply altered life experience requires nothing less than a revealing by the Spirit. Revealed hope must be greater than our biggest faith challenge, greater than our darkest disappointment. Revealed hope is greater because the person in the relationship—Jesus—is greater. While fear restricts relationships, hope enlarges our relationship. Jesus encompasses the entire authentic hope spectrum.

New heart revelation also involves our mental processing of information. As we mull over new ideas, at some point the light comes on for us. It is the "Aha!" moment. Ideas and concepts fit together in a way that we have never seen before. This is the enjoyment of discovery in a new perspective on hope. Change in core beliefs includes processing new information into a new way of thinking, a new transcendent way of experiencing life

## Summary

Some foundational thoughts that we are considering:

Transcendent Hope

- Transcendence is an aspect of hope
- The transcendent joins innate hope in energizing destiny
- Transcendence is in DNA
- Continued, secure relational attachment is vital for hope
- Beyond learning, transcendent hope comes from experience
- Innate, core beliefs develop into persuasions
- Core beliefs may be healthy or toxic
- Core beliefs are foundational to life relationships
- 'Knowing" dimension of hope comes by revelation
- Revelation is a key to the fullness of hope

Some key scriptures for this section:

> Proverbs 23:18; Ecclesiastes 9:4; Psalms 22:9; Ephesians 1:18-19; Romans 4:18, 5:3, 8:24-25; I Corinthians 2:9-12

## LET'S CONNECT TO DISCUSS THIS CHAPTER:

**Join My Interactive Discussions:** Please come visit with me at www.IncreaseHope.com in section "Book Resources" where I will be posting specifically for this chapter. I invite you to leave your comments or questions and I'll personally be responding. I will also have audios and videos and other resources pertinent to the topics in this chapter.

**Join Our Live Events:** Carol and I also offer special events www.HopeAcceleratorSeminars.com for more personal and in-depth face to face training and equipping. I look forward to continued connection with you.

Blessings! - Arnold J. Allen

## Personal Notes

Hope tempers pain, and as we sense less pain, that feeling of hope expands, which further reduces pain.

*But we have this treasure in earthen vessels, that the excellence of the power may be of God and not of us,*

II Corinthians 4:7 (NKJV)

# 4
# Physical Hope

## The Connection of Body and Mind

One of the challenges of giving definition to authentic hope is separating it from the system of which it is a part. Hope is part of an intricate network of internal and external relationship. It is in our heart, our mind, our soul, and "in the bones." Our physical makeup, our mental/emotional capabilities, and the spiritual dimension within us hold an energy that influences how life unfolds. Dr. Groopman gives this account of his own personal journey into the reality of the physical power of hope.

I was most intrigued by the sense that I may have felt physical changes caused by hope. But I distrusted my impression. So I asked, as a scientist, is there a biological mechanism whereby the feeling of hope can contribute to clinical recovery? And if there is such a biology of hope, how far is its reach and what may be its limits?

In the mid '90s, I returned to school to complete a graduate degree in counseling. Although Groopman had not written *The Anatomy of Hope* at that time, the type of questions he pursues and his idea of "a biology of hope" were some of my own interests. In addition to biology or physical hope, I desired an understanding of the psychology and spirituality of hope. I wanted answers to: How is hope understood in the whole person? How are these various perspectives joined to each other?

I had served 18 years in Youth With A Mission (YWAM), a Christian mission agency. My role focused on pastoral care and staff development for our workers and leaders. During this time, I encountered a situation with a staff member that was beyond my training and experience. A number of mental illnesses had disrupted her life, her family and the mission training community for which she and her husband provided leadership. Since I was a primary resource person in the Canadian division of YWAM, it was up to me to deal with this situation. Often this particular mental illness—psychosis—has a variety of bazaar faces, as was the case with this person. Working closely with her family doctor and other professionals, we eventually helped the family transition to a less stressful environment. She found healing and returned to a relatively normal life.

Faced with an overwhelming challenge, I needed answers, not just for working with mental illness, but to understand the relationship between the physical, mental, emotional and spiritual dance that comprises human beings, whether in illness or wellness. As I worked with this situation, I continued on a journey gaining insight beyond the casual magazine accounts of mind-body connections. In the back of my mind were the fledgling ideas on hope that eventually matured and are presented here. In my search, I wanted more, needed more, looked for more. Is there a "grid of truth," I wondered, developed from science to govern or at least, guide diagnosis and recovery? Can one overcome a disease or condition—mental, physical or spiritual—through thinking differently, or making positive confession, or generating enough positive desire and gut determination to achieve victory?

Carol and I had encountered accounts of unexpected remissions of dreaded diseases through positive confession of wellness. Was it possible to create a way of believing—a psychology of wellness—based on these accounts? Yet, how many people had confessed and still suffered from their diseases?

Through decades of helping friends and clients wrestle with a variety of afflictions, we experienced some amazing demonstrations of healing and deliverance. But we also experienced the grief, disappointment, and burden of the loss of various battles for deliverance and healing. Dr. Groopman shares that experience as he encountered it in people trying to justify why folks were not healed through mind-over-body thinking:

> The reason that visualization and meditation failed to eradicate breast cancer or lymphoma or a brain tumor was that (according to the positive thinking folks) the afflicted individual was not doing it well enough; he was holding on to anger and depressive thoughts that had activated the malignancy. These negative emotions blocked the salutary effects of positive thinking. In essence, invoking a mind-body connection in this way blamed the victim for his own malady and ultimately for his demise.

In my pursuit of understanding and insight, I did not want to blame the victim nor "throw the baby out with the bath water"— if indeed there was a baby to be kept. While I have experienced what Groopman is talking about, many accounts suggested that there is more to holistic wellness than I knew. Scripture affirms the spirit-soul-mind-body connection as it addresses the "inner man," the "outer man," the mind and spirit in the body.

> *Beloved, I pray that you may prosper in all things and be in health, just as your soul prospers.*
>
> III John 1:2 (NJKV)

> *Therefore we do not lose heart, but though our outer man is decaying, yet our inner man is being renewed day by day.*
>
> II Corinthians 4:16 (NASB)

Maintaining my ignorance, the link of mind, spirit, soul and body was not addressed in a holistic manner during my either my theological or psychological education. Occasionally, vague references to some parallels came up in discussion, but generally, the conversations caused suspicion over being a "new age proponent."

## Inner-man Meets Outer-man

In my search, I found that modern Psychology suggests that stress, anxiety and depression have physical effects, and that people get well by dealing with these issues. In contrast, many theologians address the spiritual issues, dealing with unforgiveness, bitterness and resentment to foster wellness.

Although each of these contributing factors is important, there seemed to be more to the solution. Rarely were positive emotions such as hope suggested as an influence altering in combating illness and restoring wellness.

Determined to understand more, the objectives in my pursuit of the role of hope in wellness included:

- to discover how hope is manifest in the whole person
- to understand the manifestation of hope as a physical influence
- to determine if hope or chemistry is the influencer of physical issues of the body.

I soon realized that I could trim my objectives down simply by choosing an Eastern view of mankind over the Western approach. This view considers the human being as one unit. The inner man and the outer man are simply two views of the same thing. A person does not have a body, as the Greeks taught, but instead *is* an animated body, a unit of life manifesting itself in fleshly form, a mental/physical organism with a resident spirit. The Greek thinking approach tends to be dualistic: the body is an entity in and of itself; the mind, including emotion, thoughts, perceptions, reflections and desires is a separate entity. Modern medicine and psychology is based primarily upon the Greek mindset and generally leaves the idea of the "soul or spirit" for the theologians to sort out.

Scripture—especially the New Testament—uses various terms to describe aspects of the inner man and the outer man. In addition, psychology, theology and biology each develop their own terms for describing various ideas and activities. Therefore, to make the discussion of authentic hope relevant as possible, it is essential that the various terms remain part of the discussion. Regarding terminology, I propose an open-minded stance at this stage of deliberation.

## Our Belief Effects Our Result

My search for a grid of truth considered the influence of hope on the physical person. As it turned out, the sugar pill or placebo effect/response was one of the intriguing areas of study that I encountered in grad school. Interestingly, one key historical event significantly influenced the use of placebo in the US. During World War II, Dr. Henry Beecher was tending to injured US troops under bombardment from the German Army. When morphine supplies ran low, an army nurse told a wounded patient that he was receiving a huge shot of helpful medication when in fact he was receiving a simple salt water injection. To Dr. Beecher's surprise, the injection had the same effects as morphine—it relieved the patient's immense pain and stopped him from falling deeper into shock. Later in the U.S., Beecher published his experience and initiated a new approach to testing drugs.

The study of the placebo response is the study of how expectations, beliefs and values shape brain processes. Further, it examines how brain processes are related to perception, emotion and ultimately, mental and physical health. In essence, it seeks to understand how a placebo influences our mental or physical activities—positively or negatively. Can our way of thinking, our expectation or feeling impact illness and wellness?

A holistic view of mankind from the Biblical perspective

considers the physical, mental/emotional and spiritual as all combined. This holistic view is clearly confirmed by the placebo response. The whole person—the entire being—is involved in response to a stimulus, whether real or imaginary. Belief and expectation—two basic parts of hope—were also key elements to the physical response of the placebo. Here is an example of the basic experiments:

- Researchers give athletes a performance enhancing drug during training, resulting in better performance.
- Prior to drug testing, a placebo (i.e. a sugar pill or a salt water injection) replaced the drug to select, unaware athletes.
- Each athlete's performance is monitored.
- The outcome of the placebo-treated athletes was compared to those continuing the drug.
- There was no measurable difference between the two groups.
- The placebo group tested clean; the drug users did not.

The placebo response demonstrates the connection between mind and body, particularly on how mental expectation assists in duplicating the drug effect.

## Not Just a Belief, a Chemical Effect

Dr. Fabrizio Benedetti, from an Italian clinic, is internationally recognized for his work with the placebo response. He has worked with the placebo response, often called Sugar Pill Effect, while researching pain. His research found that some of the test clients in his placebo groups seemed to suffer less than those on the test drugs. The drug companies considered the placebo effect little more than a nuisance.

Prior to Benedetti's research, the placebo was considered only a psychological trait related to people's hang-ups. Now, after 15 years of experimentation, he has mapped many of the placebo physical reactions. Chemicals (opioids) activated by the placebo, for example, modulate heart rate and breathing as well as relieve pain. The placebo activated brain chemical (neurotransmitter Dopamine) released by the body helps improve motor function in Parkinson's patients. Changes in brain chemicals can elevate mood, sharpen thinking ability, settle digestive disorders, and relieve insomnia, as well as limit the secretion of stress-related hormones like insulin and cortisol.

Placebo, or sugar pills, by definition have no effect, but under the right conditions they can act as a catalyst or spark. Benedetti calls this activity the body's "endogenous (internal) health care system" because the response is generated from an internal energy as opposed to an external inducement. The placebo response has noteworthy limitations. Placebo won't normally stop the growth of tumors, but it can ease the distress of chemotherapy.

## What We Think is What We Are

There is an interesting flip side of the coin in the nocebo response providing a contrasting effect. The nocebo uses the basic elements of belief and expectation that characterize the placebo. But rather than duplicating the expected positive effects of the drug, the negative side effects are demonstrated. In an example of nocebo, women who believed that they were prone to heart disease were nearly four times as likely to die of heart disease as women with similar risk factors who didn't hold such fatalistic views. The higher risk of death, in other words, had nothing to do with the usual heart disease culprits—age, blood pressure, cholesterol, or weight. Instead, it tracked closely with belief and expectation. "Think sick, be sick" cliché is often used to describe this mind-body response.

Similarly, men taking a commonly prescribed prostate drug who were informed that the medication may cause sexual dysfunction were twice as likely to become impotent as those uninformed patients. Some patients requested that the doctor not describe the side effects of the drug due to their tendency to act out the symptoms. Obviously, ignorance is not quite bliss but may avoid problems for some patients (while creating an ethical dilemma for the physician.)

## An Equal and Opposite Reaction

There certainly seems to be adequate information to demonstrate the mind-body operation of hope. Belief and expectation clearly influence some measure of physical activity. So what of the body-mind activity? Does physical wellbeing, or the lack thereof, influence one's state of hopefulness or despair? Is there a memory in the cells of the body similar to that in the brain? It does appear that there is a link between mental/emotional hope and the physical body's hope capacity. In the Eastern view of the nature of man, this active link is a given. Hope exists in spirit, soul and body. Let's look closer and see how this dance plays out.

We have lived in the northwest for about 25 years now. My siblings and most of their families still live in the same area of northern Vermont where I was born and raised.

A few years ago, I received a call that my mom was not doing well physically, and that I should return for a visit. We made the trip and spent the summer with her and family members. Mom, in her late 80s at the time, had always been very active, including a significant amount of volunteer work in the church and the community. She had received the governor's award in recognition for her community service visiting shut-ins. As we sat in her living room that summer, she described her lack of physical energy and how she was unable to care for her flower garden. The small plot in her front yard was filled to overflowing with lilies, bleeding hearts, tulips and a variety of other perennials. However, due to her inability to provide the needed care, the weeds were becoming a problem.

Mom had always planned to "live 'til she died," meaning that she would rather be dead than not be able to do the things that she enjoyed. Gardening, high school basketball games and the annual family trip to the Maine seacoast were not negotiable. At that time, I think there were well over 100 family members of her immediate offspring. Most of the sports teams in the area usually had a family member's involvement or influence. There was a lot to live for, but due to congestive heart failure, she simply did not have the energy to keep up her personal and community activity. Her hope of continuing the life that she enjoyed was fading along with her body. With a very strong, settled faith that assured her afterlife, we certainly did not want her on this earth any longer than she wanted to be here. But maybe her "want to" could be changed so she could enjoy life more, and her family and friends could enjoy her a little longer.

With the encouragement of family, she eventually gave oxygen a try. Almost immediately she began to feel better. Soon, she was back in the garden and filling her schedule up with the activities that she so enjoyed. The shift in her physical sense of wellness contributed to her desire to live longer. The expectation of a fulfilling life was renewed as her body told her that she could do more. My mom lived for another two and one half years. Just a few days before she passed away, she sat in my sister's living room teaching some great grandchildren how to knit. She was "living 'til she died"! She had hope to the end.

## Our Bodies Remember

Concerning the body's contribution to the hope equation, some very informative and helpful research is being done with organ transplant patients. An eight-year-old girl, who received the heart of a murdered ten-year-old girl, began having vivid and recurring nightmares about the murder. The detailed descriptions of the murderer, given by the recipient to the police, were used to find and convict the man, who had murdered the donor. The girl knew when the murder happened. She identified the weapon used to kill her donor. She was able to describe many details, including the place of the murder, the clothing he wore, what the little girl he killed had said to him. Everything the little heart transplant recipient reported was completely accurate. While such claims may appear to be outlandish, there may be a reasonable explanation for them.

Further intrigue is found in Claire Sylvia's book *A Change of Heart*, in which she writes of a man named Tim, whose heart she had received. Following her transplant, she reported having acquired his love for particular foods and drinks that had not been her desire prior to the transplant. Sylvia found herself changing her clothing preferences from bright reds and oranges to cool colors. Becoming more aggressive and impetuous, she began expressing the personality of her donor.

Liver transplant patients report changes in food preferences, attitudes toward children and music choices. Following surgery, some have become more talkative and quicker to express opinions that were kept private prior to surgery. One transplant patient seemed to connect with the donor's happy childhood experience. She discovered her dream of a young girl on a swing in a farm setting was an actual account of her donor's life. A donor's preferences seemed to influence the kidney recipients experience as she reported a desire for new foods and an interest in new hobbies.

Obviously, not all transplant recipients experience notable levels of emotional or mental change from organs. Yet, dozens of reports exist with accounts similar to these. While researchers have not discovered an approach to track and verify the body-mind link of organ recipients, it is helpful to recognize that an information/communication line exists. For the purpose of this book, I simply want to affirm the reality that, to some measure, body parts send memos to the mind, and that these messages carry an influence. The memos are part of the outer-man/inner-man link. Hope will tend to increase or diminish depending upon the message of the body parts.

Dr. Groopman gives this perspective related specifically to the measurable physical effects of pain and the chemical activity in the brain:

This is the vicious cycle. When we feel pain from our physical debility, that pain amplifies our sense of hopelessness; the less hopeful we feel, the fewer endorphins and enkephalins and the more CCK (brain related chemicals) we release. The more pain we experience due to these neurochemicals, the less able we are to feel hope. To break that cycle is key. It can be broken by the first spark of hope: Hope sets off a chain reaction. Hope tempers pain, and as we sense less pain, that feeling of hope expands, which further reduces pain. As pain subsides, a significant obstacle to enduring a harsh therapy is removed.

Although my mom did not have to face a harsh cancer therapy, Dr. Groopman's point seems quite applicable in explaining the shift in her attitude toward living longer. As she felt better, she had more desire to reengage with her loved activities. The renewed engagement in enjoyable activities increased her energy rather than expended it, resulting in the strength to do more.

## Review

Thus far in this chapter, I have presented the activities of the physical body as the biology of hope. Some chemical and physical feelings are clearly a response to expectation and belief. Emotions are generally discussed as an aspect of the mind. In reality, emotions are manifest as an aspect of the whole person: spirit, soul and body. For the sake of discussion, we can consider the activity of the mind as central to the psychology of hope. I will usually discuss emotions from a mental point of reference simply because that is how they are thought of in general. As we look at the dynamic flow of the spirit, other aspects of emotions will come to light.

An increased understanding and insight into the physical biology of hope, mental/emotional, psychology of hope and spirituality of hope is essential in developing a "grid of truth." This establishes a reference for hope-filled strategies in various situations. The trauma of war, the miscarriage or abortion of a child, shifting the roots of depression or altering sources of suicidal thoughts may all find a hidden resource in the hope factor. As we embrace a Hebrew view (thus a Biblical view) of the human being, we also will embrace the role of the spirit in the authentic hope equation.

## Summary

Some aspects of hope considered in this chapter:

- We can build a "grid of truth" to understand and develop hope.
- There is a physical biology of hope, a mental and emotional psychology of hope, and a spirituality of hope.
- Hope is more than positive confession.
- A Hebrew view of mankind considers the whole being as one unit—the "inner man" and the "outer man.'
- Placebo and nocebo responses have very powerful influences on the whole person.
- There is a memory of some type in the cells of the body, especially the major organs, not just in the brain.
- Body parts send messages to the mind as part of the outer-man/inner-man link which influences hope.

- Hope has a significant influence on the body.

Some Scriptures considered in this chapter:

III John 1:2 NJKV,  II Corinthians 4:7; 4:16 NASB

## LET'S CONNECT TO DISCUSS THIS CHAPTER:

**Join My Interactive Discussions:** Please come visit with me at www.IncreaseHope.com in section "Book Resources" where I will be posting specifically for this chapter. I invite you to leave your comments or questions and I'll personally be responding. I will also have audios and videos and other resources pertinent to the topics in this chapter.

**Join Our Live Events:** Carol and I also offer special events www.HopeAcceleratorSeminars.com for more personal and in-depth face to face training and equipping. I look forward to continued connection with you.

Blessings! - Arnold J. Allen

*Personal Notes*

_____
_____
_____
_____
_____
_____
_____
_____
_____
_____

Authentic hope is an intimate partnership of our whole person with the Spirit of God. Spirit-to-spirit activity with our entire being is God's intention.

*For what man knows the things of a man except the spirit of the man which is in him? Even so no one knows the things of God except the Spirit of God.*

I Corinthians 2:11 (NKJV)

# 5
# The Breath

## The Heart's Flowing Energy

A vineyard once stored new wine in a cellar alongside old wine. Interestingly, the old wine, which had settled over the years, began to respond to the aging activity of the new wine. Apparently, there is a working activity that occurs as new wine ages. Somehow, the presence of the working new wine activated a new working in the old, settled wine.

Like the new wine in the cellar, the activity of our personal spirit influences our being. The personal spirit's energy manifests as activity in and around the body and soul. In addition, the Holy Spirit is actively "working" our whole person: body, soul and spirit. We could view the soul as the wine, and the body as the bottle. The spirit may be considered as the invisible activity in both the wine and the atmosphere. The spirit fills the container—our living flesh—with its energy.

*And the Lord God formed man of the dust of the ground, and breathed into his nostrils the breath of life; and man became a living soul.*

Genesis 2:7 (KJV)

Scripture will sometimes describe man in two parts: "inner man" and "outer man." At other times, the whole person is referenced as three parts: body, soul and spirit.

Bible teacher, Harold Eberle, describes the relationship of the spirit and soul this way:

> When I talk about the spirit as an entity apart from the soul, I am speaking of that spiritual energy which originated from the breath of God, yet now resident within a person. When I speak of the spirit/soul, I am talking about the two elements that function together as one. When I talk about the soul only, I am doing this for the purpose of understanding; but please keep in mind that the soul does not exist independently of the spirit which sustains it.

*Spiritual Realities*, pg. #80

In this chapter, we will consider the influences and activities of the individual's spirit as well as the Spirit of God, as they relate to authentic hope. To help keep these activities separate in this discussion, I will capitalize "Spirit" when referring to God's Spirit. I will also use the term "atmosphere" to emphasize the activity of the personal spirit. The energy that generated activity in the wine in the cellar was both inside the containers and around them. The personal spirit functions within the framework of our personal atmosphere—our own wine cellar.

## Hope in the Mind, Body and Spirit

It is challenging to find ways to explain and clarify these separate yet intertwined activities. Imagine a third-grader discussing the atmosphere in which photosynthesis, germination and metamorphosis take place. We can grasp the general idea, but there is still a lot to discover. In like manner, there will always be a degree of mystery in the activities of the spirit and Spirit. The results are observable but not easily explained.

As we saw in the study on the effects of placebos, some activities in nature are never fully explained independent of the spirit of life and hope. The spirit does not function according to natural laws, thus natural comparisons can never give us the whole picture of spiritual activities. Certainly, science can help us with some aspects of hope. However, authentic hope requires that we gain insight into the spiritual atmosphere in which it operates.

With this understanding, we can now take a fresh look at some of the aspects of hope presented earlier—the amazing activities of the physical and biological nature of hope. Hope, manifesting as belief, expectation or anticipation has a profound influence on the activities of our body, releasing brain stimulating chemicals that significantly influence our quality of life.

The converse is also true. Feelings of wellness or illness in the body impact the quality of hope. Cellular memory—the idea that organs hold personal information—impacts the activity of hope.

We also briefly considered the relationship between thoughts and emotions to understand the psychology of hope. Thoughts bring responses in the body and are the primary initiators of emotions. Authentic hope, therefore, manifests a very powerful role in both thoughts and emotion.

Spiritual hope is the activity of hope in the personal spirit and the influence of the Spirit interacting with us. We will examine various aspects of the dynamic interplay of spirit, soul, and body. We will further consider the interaction of the Spirit with our whole being. We are spiritual beings who are originated and sourced from *the* Spiritual Being. To summarize:

- The Psychology of Hope involves the mind, thoughts and emotions.
- The Biology of Hope involves the body, emotions and physical feelings.
- The Spirituality of Hope involves the spirit, emotions and Spirit activity.

## The Working Energy

Beyond belief, anticipation and expectation—and in the context of relationship—hope is also an energy flow. By design, we are not only mental/physical beings but also spirit/physical beings and spirit/mental beings. Because of our connectivity, any activity in one area of our being influences the whole.

The flow of life and hope create synergy. "The sum of the whole is greater than its parts" fits well here. Physical energy coupled with emotional and mental energy, is intertwined with the energy of the spirit. Authentic, spiritual hope is a dynamic part of the living, innate energy harnessing the physical, mental and emotional elements of our nature as we move into the unfolding future.

The Spirit, as a personal being, constantly interacts with our spirit. The Father, Jesus and the Holy Spirit each, and as one, are actively bestowing life in individuals as well as in families, people-groups and nations. Our current discussion will focus on the individual.

Proverbs 4 talks about the expression of active energy:

> Watch over your heart with all diligence, for from it flow the springs of life.

> Proverbs 4:23 (NASB)

It is helpful to see that this life-flow includes the dynamic nature of hope. While the personal spirit sustains life in the soul and body, hope is the future-orientation of that life. The energy of hope is continuously directing the soul and body toward a promising future. Therefore, the quality of our future is governed by the quality of our hope. As described in Chapter 1, it is a relational hope by design, as illustrated by the exchange between Carol and her granddaughter, Autumn, which carried an expectation based on the relationship of the giver and receiver.

## Value of the Personal Spirit

The relational aspect of hope includes a connectedness to the Spirit. All life source—thus all hope—flows from the very person of God into each and every living being. The degree in which an individual engages and develops that life-flow equals the quality of hope. There will always be hope as long as there is life. More life-flow; more hope-flow! This is an important point that we will pursue throughout our study. For now, it is helpful to see that the spirit and the Spirit sustain the individual connectedness to the future for the body and soul.

Alas, the existence and activity of the personal spirit is often denied, ignored or discounted. Yet our ignorance of the spirit does not change the reality of its existence and activities. Although the personal spirit has been part of humans since Adam, many schools of thought have convinced learners that it does not exist, comparing it to the effects of a placebo.

In truth, our spirit is often the first informer and responder as we encounter new situations, such as the spiritual sense when someone walks into the room unnoticed. At times, we may become aware of someone watching us and turn to see who may be there. While some individuals are much more in tune with this aspect of life, each and every person is spiritual. As the scripture states:

> *For who among men knows the thoughts of a man except the spirit of the man which is in him?*
>
> I Corinthians 2:11a (NASB)

> *If there is a natural body, there is a spiritual body.*
>
> I Corinthians 15:44b (NASB)

The activities of the spirit and the mind are separate yet connected. The spirit enables the knowing. Similar to the old wine responding to the activity of the new wine, the spirit gathers information. Enabled by its flowing nature, the spirit knows what is happening in the mind and body. Expectation, anticipation and belief—key elements of hope—are in the spirit as well as the mind and body.

# The Heart, The Deepest Center

By nature, mature hope is more intuitive, integrative, and holistic than logical, sectional and sequential; it is more imaginative than analytical. The many facets of hope are beyond the reach of our reasoning abilities. Walking in a hopeful posture has more to do with a creative heart than a reasoning mind. Although a very strong mental process is active in hope, the intuitive element is even more fundamental. Hope isn't as concerned with common sense as it is with "heart sense."

Throughout our being, there is a spirit of hope, a soul of hope and a body of hope, integrated and superimposed one upon the other. The center of this integrated being is the heart. The Greek word for heart, *kardia*, also means "the core or center." The heart is the core of a person, the deepest center of our being. Let's look at the scripture quoted above in the light of our current understanding.

> *Watch over your heart with all diligence, for from it*
> *flow the springs of life.*
>
> Proverbs 4:23 (NASB)

As life flows, so hope flows. Hope flows from the heart, the core of our being. While it is clear from scripture that many positive and negative characteristics flow from the heart, for the purpose of our study, we will focus mostly on the positive heart activity of hope.

*Whoever believes in me, as the Scripture has said, rivers of living water will flow from within them. By this He meant the Spirit.*

John 7:38-39 (NIV)

A central activity of the heart is to develop and maintain relationship with the Spirit of God. Although the Spirit may be active in a specific part of our being, the heart is most central. As mentioned earlier, the degree to which an individual engages and develops that life-flow equals the quality of hope. As we come to know the life-giving Spirit through Jesus, a new dimension of hope and life opens to us. As Paul says:

*For in him, we live and move and have our being.*

Acts 17:28 (NIV)

*For by him all things were created, both in the heavens and in the earth, visible and invisible….. all things have been created through Him and for him.*

Colossians 1:16 (NIV)

## A Relationship of Intimate Hope

Although there is no question about God knowing each individual, not every person has developed the personal, intimate knowing of Him. He is the Source of hope. He is the Person of Hope! Without Him, hope would not exist.

The very core of our being, the heart, will increase its capacity for hope-flow as the relationship with the hope-Source is increased. Harold Eberle makes this point:

> The heart is the focal point of one's being. It is the
> seat of desires (Matt. 5:28), faith (Romans 10:10),
> and purpose (Acts 11:23; II Corinthians 9:7). Just as
> the physical heart pumps blood, so also the heart
> within our spirit/soul circulates the springs of life. The
> physical heart draws oxygen through the lungs, and
> food from the stomach. In a corresponding way, the
> invisible heart draws in good through holy desires
> and evil through lusts. That which is received grows
> and flows outward. The heart, then, is the core of
> the person's being, while at the same time serving
> as the fountainhead of life.
>
> This point cannot be over-emphasized enough for
> our future understanding. Wherever the heart of a
> man is pointed, his life will follow. From the heart,
> do, indeed, flow the springs of life. (ibid. p.105)

Accordingly, as the heart draws hope from various sources, our life orientation becomes increasingly hope filled. Positive thoughts, life-giving relationships, supportive medications and nutrition, and healthy environments cultivate one's hopefulness. Of course, the converse is also true. Toxic elements or impediments in these areas decrease hopefulness. The ultimate source is the living Spirit as He flows into our person.

*The Spirit Himself bears witness with our spirit.*

Romans 8:16 (NKJV)

To understand our relationship with the Spirit, we must not think of Him as a remote force or impersonal power. He is a person. He is a hope-building person (Romans 5:5). Yes, He may be quenched (1 Thessalonians. 5:19), but He is the Spirit of hope.

> *Now may the God of hope fill you with all joy and peace in believing, so that you may abound in hope by the power of the Holy Spirit.*
>
> Romans 15:13 (NASB)

Clearly, it is God's intention that all Spirit activity builds us up in energized hope by His power. This building up may be through a close encounter with God Himself. The scripture speaks of an intimate relationship through a deep connectedness to the Spirit (1 Corinthians 6:17). As with any relationship of intimacy, there is a flow involved. Harold Eberle illustrates it this way:

> I can offer a beautiful comparison by telling you about one group of people native on the North American continent who express their love for each other, not by kissing each other, but by standing very close to each other and inhaling each other's breath. This symbolizes an exchange of life between them. In similar fashion, God draws near to His people, and there is an exchange of spiritual substance, Spirit to spirit.
>
> The Greek word used in the original Bible and interpreted "inspire," literally means "to breathe into." When we speak of God inspiring something, we are saying that God has breathed in His life, energy, thoughts, authority and nature (Ibid p.119).

The initial activity of the Spirit may be experienced as a physical sensation, an emotional stirring, an upheaval of thoughts or a quickened intuitive sense. Keep in mind that we are whole beings. Therefore, the touch of the Spirit manifests in our whole person. The Spirit of hope energizes *our* expectation, anticipation and belief with *His* expectation, anticipation and belief. We become inspired, breathed into, a catalyst, facilitated, partnered, contribution to our innate hope. The activity of the Spirit is not something done *to us* as much as done *with us*. Let's define these terms to take a closer look at their meaning:

- Catalyst: stimulus to change; somebody or something that makes a change happen.
- Facilitated: simplify process; to make something easy or easier to do.
- Partnered: somebody who shares activity; one involved in an activity with someone else.
- Contribution: a role played in achieving something; the part played by someone or something in causing a result.
- Innate: integral, built in, forming an essential part of something or someone.

Authentic hope is an intimate partnership of our whole person with the Spirit of God. Spirit-to-spirit activity with our entire being is God's intention. Deuteronomy 10 commands us to serve "with all your heart and soul," and Ephesians 6:6 says we should "be doing the will of God out of soul" (YLT). The Bible emphasizes that the body is the temple in which the Spirit dwells (1 Corinthians 6:19-20). It is God's will that hope be manifest in body, soul and spirit in intimate partnership. Obviously, this level of partnering requires our cooperation. As we live in this union, the fullness of Who the Spirit is becomes an element of the partnership. This is an amazing relationship which provides us with enormous benefit.

## A Community of Embrace

My friends, Kent and Cheryl Hug, are pastors of a church in Oregon. Under their initiative and leadership, the church community has fostered a loving, healing culture. In addition to their natural born children, they have three adopted children. Cheryl shared that there came a time in her life where her energies were completely depleted. She recalls,

> When the adopted children came into our home they were very hyper, very needy and I became very worn out. The need in the children was sucking the life out of me. Becoming emotionally drained and distressed, I just couldn't get refilled. I felt isolated. At a particularly low point, I attended a Women's Aglow meeting in our city. I was feeling horrible, isolated, barely human, not alive. At one point in the meeting, I walked to the back of the room. Two of the older women that were there took one look in my eyes and knew what I needed. They simply hugged me. As they held me, something lifted off from me. It was in an instant! Life came into where I was dead. I could feel it coming into me. It was love, motherly love. I was filled with hope."

She shared further, "That is why I hug people. People need hope." I am reminded of the scripture, "Blessed be the God and Father of our Lord Jesus Christ, the Father of mercies and the God of all comfort, who comforts us in all our tribulation, that we may be able to comfort those who are in any trouble, with the comfort with which we ourselves are comforted by God" (II Corinthians 1:3-4 NKJV). Kent described a church community filled with respectful, considerate, warm, abundant hugs. Usually it is men to men or women to women but there is a freedom of warm, motherly or fatherly hugs in the fellowship. A warm, compassionate embrace is often a part of the communion celebration. Developing a community of healing that includes appropriate hugs and abundant love has resulted in many becoming free from bondages.

The community experience, described by the Hugs is a beautiful illustration of the breath of God that renews hope. As described earlier, authentic, spiritual hope is a dynamic part of the living, innate energy harnessing the physical, mental and emotional elements of our nature. When released through touch, as Cheryl describes, hope can literally flow into the dry empty places. I will further describe how this relationship plays itself out in everyday life in a later chapter.

## Summary

The concepts and ideas addressed in this chapter:

- Our personal spirit has energy.
- Energy manifests as activity in and around the body and soul.
- The Bible views man in two parts and as three parts.
- "Atmosphere" emphasizes the activity of the personal spirit.
- The spirit does not function according to natural laws.
- Spirit and spirit equals spiritual hope.

- Hope is energy, a flowing energy.
- The personal spirit is the sustaining life in the soul and body.
- Heart is the core from which life and hope flow.
- God is hope in His fundamental nature.
- Spirit becomes manifest in our whole person as a partnership activity.

Scriptures used in this chapter:

John 7:38-39 NIV; Acts 17:28; Colossians 1:16; 1 Corinthians 2:11 NJKV; Romans 5; 8:16, 10:10, 15:13 NASB; Ephesians 6:6; 1 Corinthians 6:17, 19-20 Matt. 5:28; Acts 11:23; II Corinthians 1:3-4, 9:7 Genesis 2:7 KJV; Deuteronomy 10; Jeremiah 14:8, 17:13 NIV; Proverbs 4:23 NIV

## LET'S CONNECT TO DISCUSS THIS CHAPTER:

**Join My Interactive Discussions:** Please come visit with me at www.IncreaseHope.com in section "Book Resources" where I will be posting specifically for this chapter. I invite you to leave your comments or questions and I'll personally be responding. I will also have audios and videos and other resources pertinent to the topics in this chapter.

**Join Our Live Events:** Carol and I also offer special events www.HopeAcceleratorSeminars.com for more personal and in-depth face to face training and equipping. I look forward to continued connection with you.

Blessings! - Arnold J. Allen

## Personal Notes

_____

_____

_____

_____

_____

_____

_____

_____

_____

_____

_____

_____

_____

_____

_____

_____

_____

_____

_____

_____

_____

_____

_____

_____

*Hope has an all-encompassing, pervasive power
that inspires endurance. Hope, while producing
fruit in our current life experience, remains active,
abstract and future oriented.*

*We have heard of your faith...the faith and love
that spring from the hope that is stored up for you
in heaven.*

Colossians 1:4-5 (NIV)

# 6
# Abstract Hope, Concrete Faith

## A Future Oriented Partnership

In the mid '80s, our ministry needed a facility to house a training program and provide staff housing. I considered a private girls' school campus that was coming available. Located a few miles from our other facilities, it was an ideal location. Although the buildings required a considerable upgrade, they had great potential and beautiful five-acre grounds. One afternoon, I took our family for a drive past the campus. Our daughter Amiee, 10 at the time, said that she knew it was to be ours. Back at our apartment, she immediately began to pack up the things in her room. This was her faith in action. In her heart, she knew what God was going to do in providing the campus.

At that time, I was in the hope stage of the process. I knew that God was speaking to us about a larger training facility. Still, I wondered if this was it. I did not have the same clear word from the Lord that my daughter carried. While it became clear to me later, for a while we were in different stages of revelation. She had a *faith* revelation. She knew what God was going to do. I had a *hope* revelation. I knew the desires of His heart for us to have a ministry home. But I was waiting to hear if it was to be this property. In time, I did discover God's leading and we purchased the property. Amiee was the first ready to move in!

## Hope, Faith, Love

The definitions of hope and faith are clearly displayed in the Bible but often confused in life experience. Using the word "faith" to describe the activity of both hope and faith is a common mistake, and no wonder. Until recently, I rarely met people who had heard sermons or teaching on Biblical hope. From a Biblical perspective, hope and faith are like a railroad track. Hope is one rail, faith is the other rail, and love is the rail bed grounding both. In the popular consciousness, however, hope tends to be ignored as the weaker sister of the three. Although both hope and faith are used as both nouns and verbs, our focus will be toward the verb form of each word. If you need "inspiration to endure," hope is your ticket.

## Common Grounds of Hope and Faith:

Produce the fruit of salvation and healing

Perceive the future

Characterized by anticipation

Demonstrates transcendent qualities

Described as living

Founded on the nature and character of God

## HOPE IN CONTRAST TO FAITH

| | |
|---|---|
| Remains Abstract | Bridges Abstract to Concrete |
| Pulls "Now" into the Future | Pulls the Future into "Now" |
| Sees w/ Heart & Imagination | Sees w/ Heart & Physical Eyes |
| Innate, Inborn, Pre-existing | Is imparted as a Gift |
| Fails by Dying without Heart Connection to God | Fails By Stopping Believing |
| Comes by Knowing | Comes From Hearing |
| Boundless, Abundant | Measured, Increasing |
| Primary Focus: God's Being | Primary Focus: God's Doing |
| Joined to Existing; Remains Abstract | Joined to Non-Existing, Becomes Concrete |

A simple verse in I Thessalonians gives a clear picture of the relationship of hope, faith and love.

> *We remember before our God and Father your work produced by faith, your labor prompted by love and your endurance inspired by hope in our Lord Jesus Christ*

> I Thessalonians 1:3 (NIV)

Notice how Paul connects a descriptive activity to each word. The work of God's kingdom is an activity of faith. These believers were active in bringing things from the unseen world into concrete form through the work of faith. Whether it was making tents or preaching the Good News, these people were walking it out.

The labor of the Thessalonians was characterized by love. The Greek word for labor used here means to "toil until weary" or "intense labor with troubles." Because the posture of the heart is love, a major issue in the kingdom of God concerns the heart's motive. Only one motive will qualify for God's approval: love.

The role of hope in this verse is connected to the inspiration, the energy, the driving force to endure. Without hope, they would not toil until weary. They had a heart motive of love but hope empowered the endurance. The ability to keep putting one foot in front of the other was produced by hope.

## The Abstract Connection

As Paul indicates in Romans 8, hope is always unseen. Paul says to the Romans, "hope that is seen is no hope at all" (8:24 NIV). Hope fulfilled is not the same as faith fulfilled. Faith can ultimately point to a concrete result. Again, from Romans, "Who hopes for what he already has?" (v.25).Hope has an all-encompassing, pervasive power that inspires endurance. Hope, while producing fruit in our current life experience, remains active, abstract and future-oriented. It creates the atmosphere essential to faith's operation, and so must remain active. Faith is demonstrated by the abstract becoming seen, the substance of things hoped for (Hebrews 11).

Those of us in the West tend to disregard the importance of the abstract dimension of our world. Many other cultures, especially native peoples, have a far greater level of knowledge and respect for the unseen world. The strong influence of reasoning in western thinking tends to discount the reality of the abstract.

A primary aspect of defining hope includes the abstract element. Because the Bible was written in the Middle East, it takes for granted the unseen dimension of life. Eastern thought allows for gray areas, overlaps in definition, and ideas suspended in a tension without clear lines of demarcation. And while hope, faith and love all share the abstract dimension in some measure, authentic hope remains the most elusive to the concrete, reasoning mind.

## Hope: The Soul's Anchor

Hope, in contrast to faith, connects with things that already exist. This is in sharp conflict to how most people think about hope. Far from a wispy element, hope is an anchor to the soul (Hebrews 6:19). An anchor attaches to a very solid place. Authentic, Biblical hope attaches to the character of God. God's character and ways are well established and immovable. They exist and do not change. Obviously, hope and faith share the common ground of the character and nature of God. However, the primary manifestation of each is different.

Authentic hope is attached to the most secure place in existence—the very presence of God. The most intimate of relationships is represented by the holy of holies behind the veil. The New Living Translation states:

> This hope is like a strong and trustworthy anchor for

*our souls. It leads us through the curtain of heaven into God's inner sanctuary. Jesus has already gone there for us He has become our eternal High Priest in the line of Melchizedek.*

Hebrews 6:19-20 NLT

## Boundless Hope

Biblical faith has defined boundaries while hope is limitless. "Think of yourself with sober judgment, in accordance with the measure of faith God has given you" (Romans 12:3b NIV). There is a measure, a metron, a sphere of influence or power that is associated with Biblical faith. One dictionary of New Testament words defines this dimension as "that which is measured, a determined extent, a portion measured off." It is clear that God intends that we continue to grow in faith (II Cor.10:15). It is clear that, at any given time, we are living within a certain measure of faith. Hope, on the other hand, does not have the same parameters. We may limit our own hope but the scripture calls us clearly to put our abundant hope in God.

*I pray that God, the source of hope, will fill you completely with joy and peace because you trust in him. Then you will overflow with confident hope through the power of the Holy Spirit.*

Romans 15:13 NLT

The Message Bible presents this view:

*Oh! May the God of green hope fill you up with joy, fill you up with peace, so that your believing lives,*

*filled with the life-giving energy of the Holy Spirit,*
*will brim over with hope!*

Paul is praying for an abundant overflow of hope. Clearly, the abundance of hope provides an atmosphere where faith can operate.

The room I am writing in has an abundance of oxygen. I am using some, Carol is using some, and the fire in the fireplace is using some. There is more than enough. The atmosphere of hope is similar in its relationship to faith. There is more than enough confidence in the character of God, more than enough expectation of His showing up, more than enough sense of His favor. Faith uses what it needs and there is still more!

## The Hope Of Jabez

Declarations and confessions of hope are vital to the growth and development of faith. *The Prayer of Jabez*, by Bruce Wilkinson, is a good example of a declaration of hope. He describes the general, future blessings of God that characterize hope.

> *And Jabez called on the God of Israel saying, "Oh,*
> *that You would bless me indeed, and enlarge my*
> *territory, that Your hand would be with me, and that*
> *You keep me from evil, that I may not cause pain."*
> *So God granted him what he requested.*
>
> I Chronicles 4:10 (NKJV)

Jabez's prayer is a quest for blessing, enlarging, and keeping. It fits well within the Biblical definition of hope, the confident expectation of the good release of God. Jabez is not asking for something specific but a general blessing. This is a prayer that expresses the confidence that God will show up and bless his family. In the atmosphere of expectation, God demonstrates His goodness.

Faith is expressed in substance while hope is expressed in non-substance. As Hebrews 11:1 (NIV) describes, substance first exists as non-substance. "Faith is the substance of things hoped for, the evidence of things not seen."

As a young pastor in the early 1970s, it was a challenge to understand and apply the confession of faith doctrine that was rapidly influencing parts of the church. At the time, I was in a conservative denomination that strongly encouraged faith but had difficulty with the "name it, claim it" part of the faith movement. This is the spiritual equivalent to what I described in Chapter 5 with the mind over body, positive thinking approach.

Although I possessed a passion to have all that God intended for my church and my family, and while much of what was being proclaimed was clearly Biblical, something didn't sit right with me. The confession of faith remained a source of tension until I came to an understanding of Biblical hope. Then I realized that most of the "faith confession" was actually a hope confession. All of the promises of God should be confessed and affirmed as our future. We are to express both a faith confession and a hope confession. Every unfulfilled promise of God is in my future. In hope, we proclaim all that God is and intends to be among His people. He is everything that He says He is, and He will demonstrate that to each of His children in His way and time.

## Affirming Hope Confession

So what is a Hope confession? Hebrews 4:14 in the Amplified Bible reads, "let us hold fast to our confession." To clarify understanding, these and other translators added "[of faith in Him]." There is no basis in the text for this addition. This term "hold" means to be strong, to prevail in a teaching or a tradition. The focus of the confession is Jesus. The encouragement is to confess or profess Him. We are to profess the truth, according to Scripture, of who God is as revealed in the Word. Our confession is a "holding fast" to the nature and character of God.

A further understanding is given in Hebrews:

> Let us hold unswervingly to the hope [elpis] we profess, for he who promised is faithful.

> Hebrews 10:23 (NIV)

Some translations have mistakenly used the word "faith" for the Greek word *elpis* in this verse. This term clearly means hope. The focus of our hope confession is Jesus, the faithful promiser. (For more on this point, see Appendix B.)

Confess! Confess! Confess! Affirm! Affirm! Affirm! The promises, ways and character of God cannot be confessed or affirmed too much. There is a significant function for those who pray the Jabez Prayer. The prayer is for an increase of the expectancy of God's activity in one's life. Authentic Biblical hope is clearly as powerful as Biblical faith. (I Cor. 13:13)  Hope simply has a different role and leads to a different result.

A balanced walk with God requires both truths to mature in our experience. When one truth is lacking, the whole walk is out of balance and less fruitful. There is a restful relationship between faith and hope. When faith becomes restless, we are forced back to *what God has said*. However, when we lose hope and become anxious, we are forced back to the *ONE WHO IS!* This distinction is essential to maintaining our spiritual well-being.

Authentic, Biblical hope includes expectation, anticipation and belief in our relationship with God. Further, His nature and character become manifest in all our relationships as we confidently, expectantly celebrate life. When God is manifest, our situation is impacted. Hope is life changing!

## Faith Needs Hope

Hope always moves toward what it anticipates, knows and trusts. It does not move in the sense of leaving. It is more of a shift of focus and activity towards something. To think of this relationship as a moving away from hope may confuse the reality of each truth.

While hope and faith share some common ground in anticipating the activity of spirit and Spirit, faith requires an impregnation of hope. Then God's contribution creates a complete change in our experience. In the process, hope remains the expectation, anticipation and belief that the goodness of God will continue to become manifest as the activity of faith unfolds. One expression can be seen, the other expression remains abstract. Hope is always the same while faith is continually changing.

> *Faith makes us sure of what we hope for and gives us proof of what we cannot see.*
>
> Hebrews 11:1 CEV

## The Quickening

When I am sick, I need to be healed. Because I have living faith in the Lord Jesus Christ, I can place my hope in the promise of healing. I know Him, His character and nature as healer. As I focus on this hope, my hope and faith run parallel. As the plan of God unfolds, the Lord quickens my spirit, manifests His word into my hope and I am healed.

The word of God says that I am healed by His stripes. As this word is heard by my spirit from the Spirit, the fruit of it manifests in my body. What we "hope for" is in our heart, unseen. Faith makes it seen and concrete.

God is the One who speaks. He is the One who we need to press in to for the discovery of what is holding up healing or help in any other area of need. One thing is certain, there is a place that we can go, in Him, for comfort and understanding. Hope is the "cleft in the Rock" where we can get out of the storm and wait for God to show up (Exodus 33:22). When our faith reaches its limit we can, in hope, slip into the cleft to refocus, worship and re-establish the resting place for faith and love.

In a certain ministry season of our lives, we had a vision to mobilize children into outreach ministry. This desire was not just to minister to children but to find a way for them to impact the world with their lives. God's heart to express His life through children became our heart. When He spoke to our team, "Make room for children in the ministry," our expectant hope received His word and joined faith in our hearts. By faith, children brought life to festivals, prisons, convalescent homes and the streets. By faith, people were healed, saved and encouraged. The unseen took on costumes, music, three thousand sandwiches and a hundred venues. Our hope and His vision became history making faith.

## Amari Faith

In the reality of the everyday journey of life, hope, faith and love are as interconnected as body, soul and spirit. It is essential to define, describe and demonstrate the activity of hope in a synergetic relationship with love and faith. There are times in the journey that demonstrate the beauty and power of that synergy. I am reminded of the scripture that says "A cord of three strands is not quickly broken" (Ecc. 4:12 NIV). A quality life journey includes the full expression of the hope, faith and love synergy.

The journey of critical illness demands the powerful synergy of this trinity. Tim and Sarah, parents of Amari Faith, experienced the life-sustaining force of that synergy. Following a very intense season surrounding her birth, Amari grew as a beautiful baby. At about three and one half months, Sarah noticed the baby's tummy seemed rather hard. After trying a variety or measures to ease the problem, she knew there was something more going on. The doctor requested an ultrasound and scheduled it for the following day. As Sarah drove home from the visit, she felt the strong urgency that the procedure needed to happen immediately, not the next day as planned. Although there had been no room in the schedule, she phoned the office. The receptionist informed her that at that very moment, they were receiving a cancelation. She took the opening immediately.

The experienced technician called another tech and a doctor to check out what appeared to be an enlarged organ. They immediately decided to send her to the Seattle Children's Hospital, about 2 hours away. The instructions: "Amari is to have nothing by mouth," gave Sarah the sense that this was a life or death situation. A very unrestful night followed. The next day at Children's further tests and scans confirmed a 12 cm (nearly 5 inch) malignant tumor had grown inside one kidney. When the doctor wanted to wait for the surgery, Sarah's response to the nurse was, "Have that doctor come down to this room, look at my baby and tell me that she needs to wait!" She needed to stand strong on Amari's behalf. Her name means "promised by God" and Sarah knew in her heart she was God's gift to their family.

In Sarah's own words:

> It was "hope against hope." I'm going to believe God no matter what the circumstances. I felt numb, kind of out of my body but also a supernatural peace was with us. I didn't feel fear even though I didn't know what the outcome would be. "Come what may" – even the shadow of death – He would be with us." At one point, she walked the hall praying her utter trust. "God, I give her to you. She is yours. I put her in your arms!" The response was a settled knowing in her heart that Amari was meant to be theirs. "I knew then that I didn't need to put her back in His arms the way that I was thinking. He impressed on me that He had put Amari into my arms, she was to be ours! In my heart I said: "I can fight for that!"

Sarah did fight for Amari. From standing firm in her request for immediate, radiated blood available and in the room, to prayer releasing the kidney and tumor from the body, to commanding Amari's spirit to go back into her body following surgery, Sarah, Tim, family and friends stood together. At a distance, scores of people were joined with them for a favorable outcome.

As they prayed in the waiting room, the pager went off an hour earlier than expected. With heart pounding in her chest and thoughts whirling in her head, Sarah raced to the nurse's desk for the update. What was this call about? Great news! No blood loss! Tumor is out, completely intact! We're closing her up! We're done. She's fine! Wow! What peace filled every anxious place! Sarah looked at Tim and declared, "She does not have cancer in her body!" Although they still needed to discuss some every difficult issues, the final outcome came with the doctor's words: "She is cleared to go home!"

When Sarah did not know what the outcome would be, her heart was sustained in hope. "Even in the shadow of death He would be with us." Hope does not know the outcome but clearly knows the One who sustains. The atmosphere of hope in the heart was quick to receive and embrace faith when the Spirit quickened her spirit. At that point, she knew God was saying, "This child is yours!" It was a clear word to Sarah's heart—Amari would live. Hope focuses on who God will be to us in the journey. Faith focuses on what God is saying that He is doing in the journey. Love transcends both hope and faith. Sarah's motive from beginning to end expressed the powerful passion of love. The synergy of the three stranded cord, hope, faith and love, became manifest as the family walked through the difficulty.

Although it has been only a few months since the surgery, the medical staff are confident that Amari Faith is cancer free. Tim and Sarah are confident that their "gift of God" is destined for a long and fruitful life.

## Summary

Some things that we are considering about the Biblical relationship of hope and faith:

- Hope and faith are often confused.
- Hope and faith share some common ground in spiritual activity.
- Hope attaches to what is now in existence of God's character, yet remains abstract.
- Faith connects to what is not yet in existence, but will come into a concrete form or characteristic.
- Faith is given in measure.
- Hope is boundless.
- Faith is about getting things done & can be seen.
- Hope is concerned with the personal being & remains unseen to the natural eye.
- Confession of hope & faith are both important and essential to growth and fruitfulness.
- Faith is always changing, hope remains the same.

Some scriptures to consider:

Exodus 33:22; I Chronicles 4:10; Ecclesiastes 4:12; Colossians 1:4-5; Romans 8:24-25, 12:3, 15:13; I Corinthians 13:13; II Corinthians 10:15; I Thessalonians 1:3; Hebrews 4:14, 6:19-20, 10:23, 11:1.

## LET'S CONNECT TO DISCUSS THIS CHAPTER:

**Join My Interactive Discussions:** Please come visit with me at www.IncreaseHope.com in section "Book Resources" where I will be posting specifically for this chapter. I invite you to leave your comments or questions and I'll personally be responding. I will also have audios and videos and other resources pertinent to the topics in this chapter.

**Join Our Live Events:** Carol and I also offer special events www.HopeAcceleratorSeminars.com for more personal and in-depth face to face training and equipping. I look forward to continued connection with you.

Blessings! - Arnold J. Allen

## *Personal Notes*

_____   _____
_____   _____
_____   _____
_____   _____
_____   _____
_____   _____
_____   _____
_____   _____
_____   _____
_____   _____
_____   _____
_____   _____
_____   _____
_____   _____
_____   _____
_____   _____
_____   _____
_____   _____
_____   _____
_____   _____
_____   _____
_____   _____
_____   _____
_____   _____

Hope based on distortion produces a false reality that leads to disillusionment and hopelessness.

*Hope deferred makes the heart sick, but desire fulfilled is a tree of life.*

Proverbs 13:12 (NASB)

# 7
# Hope Deferred

## The Ultimate Wrong Question

Dealing with disappointment is as much a part of life as enjoying success. Yet, many of us expend more energy trying to live what we do not have than enjoying what we do have. Everyone has a story of a deep longing and desire that remains deferred. In some way, we all live with delay. Because of this, pain, grief and loss influence our decisions, our relationships and our perspective on the future.

It is quite amazing to stop and think about how God experiences life. Jesus lived with unimaginable pain, grief and loss. He experienced suffering beyond measure, yet He focused on the "joy set before Him" (Hebrews 12:2 NASB). He was a man of joy in the midst of distress.

We will not be without disappointments in this life; there are no easy answers. However, there is One who companions. There is One who has gone before and is now actively interceding for us as we live through affliction. There is One who values

105

the struggle as much as the prize. Because hope cannot be experienced apart from relationship with that One, we need a way of thinking that increases relationship with God.

## May

A friend, May, told me her story over lunch one day, a tale of pain in deferred hope, a deep desire put off. Divorced 16 years before, she had walked faithful to herself and God ever since.

A couple of key memories stand out to me as I reflect on her romance story.

The name Aaron was given to her in a variety of ways. Prophetic words indicated that she would meet and be joined to Aaron. Dreams and daydreams said that Aaron was to be her knight in shining armor. Friends told her that Aaron was the one. The list goes on and on with ways that Aaron was to show up in her life. Each time that a new tidbit of encouragement or information would show up, May tucked it into her heart's file labeled "Aaron."

Along with this growing anticipation came the perpetual vigilance for the "right Aaron." Each introduction to a new guy heralded a wondering if this is the one for her. If his first name wasn't Aaron, maybe his middle name would be. Details were sought. What did he look like, hair color, job, ethnic background? Does he love swing dancing the way that I do? Can he do business to compliment my career? She continually tried to satisfy the many questions arising from her dreams and various words of encouragement given to her.

With time, the burgeoning file started to smell a bit stale.

Maybe some mildew was forming on the edges wet with tears of wondering, hoping, searching and waiting. Hope was being deferred and the heart was growing sick of looking and wondering. Was this really God? Should she continue to hope or just be resigned to the loneliness of her single life?

## Inklings of Hope

Finally, the long awaited break came! In a dream, the understanding came that Aaron wasn't actually the name of the guy. The name stood for the Bible character, Aaron. There was a message in all of the subtle clues over the years. A new hope sprung forth from the grief of May's disappointment. The heart file was renamed: God's Man! The search continued with new vigor. The right guy would yet be found. The years of searching would be satisfied. She would be saved from loneliness and the sentence of imposed singleness.

May continued to share her story with me:

"A mutual friend introduced us. There was an attraction in my heart immediately. Handsome, winsome personality, right age group, the gate-keeper of my heart file immediately started the sorting process."

Hope rose as a growing volume of the file was a right fit! Over the course of the months that followed, she enjoyed the amazing discovery that his personality traits were a perfect match for hers. So many little clues seemed to add up to only one conclusion. He is the one. Yet, he remained a mystery. Were the feelings mutual? Or was I just another admirer?

The answer came as a deeply devastating blow. After not seeing him for a few weeks, a mutual friend informed her that he had moved to Australia to pursue a business opportunity and was not expected to return, ever! May spent the following days in deep grief and loss. The tears wouldn't stop. Work was left undone. He didn't even bother to say goodbye. An all too familiar, dark shadow settled on the "God's Man!" file of the heart. Hope, once again, was dashed. The dream was shattered! The heart file had been dropped in the paper shredder!

Weeks passed without a word of communication. What was going on? May's birthday arrived and was spent, not in the arms of her dream man, but in lonely contemplation and tears. Her heart longed for a sign, a word, something to lift the dark loneliness.

Finally, it came! A quick check of the email messages indicated a note from his address. In response to a forwarded email joke that she had sent months before, he had responded on her birthday! This had to be a sign from God! There could be no other explanation. Following a brief apology for not responding sooner due to the trip to Australia, he requested to have lunch when he returned in a few weeks. He was coming back! He wanted to meet! What a birthday gift! Yes! Hope soared.

Lunch came and went with no indication that she was any more special to him than any other friends. The dark cloud that had quickly blown away with the email message returned with greater darkness. May was left intensely emotional. "Was this some cruel joke from God? Was He responsible for leading me down the garden path?" Her dark eyes filled with tears as she looked intensely into mine. "Why would God jerk my heart around like this? Does He get some sort of twisted pleasure from increasing my pain, seeing my tears, leaving me empty-handed? Has my faithfulness been fruitless?"

As she sat with tears dripping from her chin as they had so many times through the seasons, my heart went out to my friend. My heart was also pierced with such an accusation of God's character. I had heard and experienced similar stories over the years as various friends, clients and acquaintances poured out the pain of deferred hope, lost love, unfulfilled dreams, longings disappointed, fears confirmed. How are we to understand this pain?

## Good News of Real Hope

It was nearly a year until May and I had a heart to heart update. In that time, she was able to put the pursuit of a husband into God's hands. Because of this, she was actually able to make a very significant shift in her heart. It came as a revelation of "God as her husband." May relinquished to God her right and desire for a husband. She discovered that in Him there was a settled place of knowing the love of God filling the need and desire to be loved. "All I ever really wanted was to be loved unconditionally. I wanted, so deeply, to be completely accepted for who I am as a woman, as a person. No strings attached. No performing and wondering if I was going to be good enough."

May has known the pain of rejection and violation. To overcome it, she needed to come into the place in God where she could give unconditionally. "It was a risk for me. I had to give God everything without strings attached. I guess I had to give Him what I really wanted in return. Actually, it turned out to be the best thing that I could do. I found a new level of love, acceptance and freedom just to be me. I could hardly believe that it was possible. I feel so free now." May went on to describe the process that felt like a hermit crab leaving a shell that it had outgrown. The crab had to leave the old place before it could find a new one—a process involving great vulnerability, and yet essential.

"You know," she continued, "after I realized that I could have such a deep relationship with God, I almost forgot about a husband. No, "forgot" isn't really the word. But the striving was gone. No more vigilance, no more "checking out the guys," always wondering when Mr. Right would arrive. I realize now that this is what God wanted for me all along." I found May describing something that I had not seen in her before—a peace, a settled serenity like a sweet perfume. Obviously, this was more than a choice. She had fallen in love with God!

My friend, May, was describing the essence of Biblical hope. "I don't know what God is going to do with me, but I know that He is with me." God wanted to fill that area of her life—knowing Him without the competition of the desire for a husband.

## Ultimate Vs. Finite Hope

Imagine life experiences going into a file system much the way you would sort information for files on your computer. The system, located in the heart, has many files. One file is infinite, ultimate, transcendent, while all of the others are finite, limited, common. One, and only one, of these files, is named "Who God Is To Me." This is not like any other heart file. Of the many other files, "Dreaming for the Right One" or as in my friend's heart, "God's Man" has to do with a special relationship. This extensive file system has a sentinel. The sentinel, as the gatekeeper of the heart files, decides where new information goes. Some thoughts, feelings, memories and pictures should not be allowed into the ultimate "Who God Is" file of the heart. This file is exclusively for revelation of God's character, nature and ways. Things that are okay for the common "Dreaming for the Right One" file don't measure up to the "Who God Is" category. These files must never get mixed up.

We sort experiences and objectives by priorities, values and significance. My friend at lunch allowed the passionate heart response to an email on her birthday to slip through to the wrong file. The passion and desire that should have gone into "Dreaming" got filed uncensored into the "Who God Is" file. "This must be God!" Passion allowed for a false value judgment. Desire distorted the real significance of the information. Loneliness shuffled the confused priorities placing a man's companionship as number one. This process made an illegitimate attachment between God's character and her wishes. "*If God really loved me, He would ............*" This is distorted thinking, misrouted experiences and objectives, skewed passion and disordered values.

This confused assortment of experiences and objectives carries a significant volume of emotional energy. Experiences generate energy in our whole being—spirit, soul and body. The greater the emotional energy, the more impact the results will have on increasing or decreasing authentic hope. This impact is increased by the personal value of the objective. For example, being a worshiper of God is high value. Choosing a life-mate, while very important, is not as high of a value. Selecting our next car is even less value than either of these two choices.

Each decision carries a measure of energy based on its priority.

Each file of experiences and objectives will be unique. They may include the failed college degree, the ruined business deal, the family feud, or the spoiled athletic accomplishment. The principle of sorting is the same as my friend's situation and needs to be worked out appropriately.

## Contaminated Hope

The things that we hope for become our vision, our dream, our future. Some hopes, visions and dreams are common and others are ultimate. The ultimate cannot be denied. The common is subject to delays, denial or reinterpretation. We need both but they have different purposes and outcomes.

The "Who God Is" file must not become contaminated. When common information ends up in an infinite, ultimate file, the resultant mix contaminates our understanding of God, resulting in fouled outcomes and deferred hope. My friend invested much of her hoping process into common content. Her recovery came as she realized the difference and sorted out her priorities.

> We exult in hope in the glory of God. And not only this, but we also exult in our tribulations, knowing that tribulation brings about perseverance; and perseverance, proven character; and proven character, hope; and hope does not disappoint, because the love of God has been poured out within our hearts through the Holy Spirit who was given to us.
>
> Romans 5:2-5 NASB

Celebrating a Biblical understanding of God's character reproduces His character in us. However, when we don't know His character or have some warped concepts of Him, our character is developed accordingly, causing us to misunderstand situations and come to wrong conclusions. Hope based on distortion produces a false reality that leads to disillusionment and hopelessness. Common hope must always be kept connected to and in the context of infinite, ultimate hope. Revelation of God's character cannot be classified the same as an email from an acquaintance, the stars lining up or a prophetic word from the pastor. Confusion of priorities is a setup for deferment and disappointment. Often, God gets the rap when we misjudge His character or contaminate our revelation of Him.

Hope deferred produces pain in the heart. No one will be without areas of deferred hope. No one will escape pain in the heart. Pain, grief and loss are common for many areas of our life experience, inescapable to some degree. Death, taxes and the pruning process are assurance of this. Fortunately, the "Who God Is" category is different.

> *"We must accept finite disappointment, but never lose infinite hope."*

> Martin Luther King, Jr.

## God Deferred?

God is never deferred in His character and ways! It may feel like He is not coming through for us. It might appear that He has not been faithful to what we have understood that He was going to do. Nevertheless, our understanding and experience are not the final authority. It is the character of God that has a category all its own. God is completely consistent in who He is, but quite unpredictable in what He will do in a given situation. "He is not a tame Lion," as C.S. Lewis says of Aslan in *The Chronicles of Narnia.*

There is a sacred place that gets filled up with a knowing of Him that is unable to be deferred. God's character transcends the character of all others. He will always be who He is! While we often do not know what He will *do* in our situation, we can always know who He will *be* in every situation. His character doesn't change.

Dreams, desires, expectations and common hopes do not always materialize the way that we want. Grief, loss, frustration and deferment may lead to hopelessness and dark despair. We might even ask, as May did, "Why is God jerking my heart around?" This idea originates in the confusion of His character with our expectations and desires. We expect things to turn out a specific way. When our anticipation doesn't materialize, emotions get the old self-talk going, creating a case of doubt against God. When our expectations are denied, frustrated or incomplete, we may conclude wrongly that God has "lead me down the garden path" and is getting a good laugh at my expense. In truth, if God leads us on a path, it is to reveal a secret place in Him, not to beat us up.

> They say, "Our bones are dried up and our hope is gone; we are cut off."

> Ezekiel 37:11 (NIV)

Certainly, loss is painful. Losing a job or bankruptcy is traumatic. Sometimes we experience a loss so pervasive that part of our heart gets frozen in pain, grief and loss. The loss of a loved one, war trauma, the responsibility for another's death, the violation of rape, or being the survivor of an attempted abortion may thrust us into a dark, cold place. These traumas carry a powerful energy all their own. At times, the flood of questions or emotion becomes overpowering. We feel as though there is no way to turn off the pain or silence, the scream of voices repeating questions without answers.

Graham Cook and a group of British Christians were establishing a new church together. The only place that they could find to meet was a room above the local pub. One particular customer of the pub was known as the town drunk. For years, he had wasted his life in a drunken stupor. During an outreach time, one of the church teenagers felt that God wanted him to speak to the drunk. A simple line, "God says that He knows what it is like to kill your own son. He killed His own son, Jesus." The man broke into deep, wailing sobs.

During the following hours, he wept himself sober. Then, the story unfolded. As a game reserve warden, he carried a gun. One evening, as he was cleaning his gun, his son came in the room and said playfully, "Daddy, shoot me." Thinking that the gun was not loaded, he pulled the trigger and killed his son. Unable to face the terrible thing that he had done, the warden remained drunk all day, every day, since the tragic accident. The teenager's word pierced deep into a place in the heart that had never been reached. Through this opening, hope created a new future. Forgiveness, in this case self-forgiveness, opened the gate to that man's future. Hope emerged.

## Cleaning Up the Mess

To lower the possibility of deferred hope, a sorting process needs to take place. The "Who God Is" file must be purged of contaminating concepts. Anything that carries a possibility of un-fulfillment must be moved to another category. Anything that can be deferred does not belong in this file. Because the absolute bottom line of authentic Biblical hope is the character of God, the sacred file in our heart must contain only the truth of who God is. The other elements of our belief system must be filed appropriately.

Occasionally, as a family, we have moved our belongings into storage for brief periods of time. A recent move included the sorting of our belongings into different categories according to priority. A few precious documents and belongings required a safety deposit box. Some important belongings were stored in a secure office. The bulk of our goods were stored in a friend's garage. Some things were put into a barn. Finally, an old 1951 Ford truck needing restoration still sits in a friend's field.

This sorting was according to value and the level of need for protection. It is this type of sorting through values and beliefs of the heart that is required to clarify our understanding of God and increase the power of hope. The very sacred place in the heart, much like the safety deposit box, has only room enough for the unchanging character and nature of God. Revelation—the disclosing of spiritual truth by the Spirit—is essential to heart understanding. Values, beliefs, memories and ideas of lesser importance must be culled from the sacred place into their own appropriate storage.

## Choosing Hope

Author and pastor, David Crone, in his book *Prisoner of Hope*, describes the power of choice in his hope journey. Following the death of his 31 year old daughter, an occasional bout of bronchitis became chronic, dangerous and unresponsive to medicines and treatments.

> Late one night, having been unable to sleep for several nights, I was fighting for air. Still in the grief of my loss, I got out of bed. Gripped by the thought that this condition was now my future, troubling questions invaded my mind and assaulted my hope.

- Is this what happens to people who lose a daughter?
- Could it be that I am going to live the rest of my life emotionally crippled by grief and physically incapacitated?
- Is my contribution to my family and my community now at an end?
- Are my dreams now dead – laying at the feet of my circumstances?

> Death, in that moment, was not my fear: living in this debilitating condition was what scared me and was pushing me toward hopelessness. Then the Holy Spirit broke through my anxiety and reminded me of the passage regarding Abraham.

> *Who, contrary to hope, in hope believed, so that he became the father of many nations…*

> Romans 4:18 (NKJV)

As I sat on the couch that night contemplating my future and staring at that verse, I realized that hope was a choice I had the power to make. Though I was struggling to breathe and ached with grief, I realized I could choose between being a prisoner of my circumstances or a prisoner of hope. I had the power to choose between being held captive by situations I seemed to have no control over, or be captivated by liberating, life-giving, faith-producing hope.

David did choose hope. He and his wife, Deborah, demonstrate the power of ultimate, authentic hope in their journey. They effectively bring hope and healing to others based on their own hope-filled choices.

Authentic Biblical hope founded on the character of God is not deferred. The essence of this hope is the person of God. When hope in another source is deferred, proper questions may help to bring understanding. Sometimes even good questions won't do it. At a time of deeply seeking God for understanding of a situation, my wife, Carol, felt the Lord say to her "Knowledge of the Holy One is understanding." Just knowing His character and ways brings us into a place of rest, beyond reach of the nagging questions, beyond the sense of abandonment and shame. Infinite, authentic hope knows no deferral.

## Summary:

Let's review how the foundation of deferred hope is built.

- We all have both infinite, ultimate objectives & common, limited objectives: God stuff, our stuff.

- We sort life experiences by priorities of the objectives: the highest is most important.
- Mix of ultimate & common contaminates our God understanding & our self-understanding.
- Wrong conclusions come from contaminated understanding.
- Our understanding & experience is not the final authority.
- God is never deferred.
- Some losses are overwhelming & pervasive.
- "Why" questions usually don't help build hope.
- Inappropriate or irrational expectations hinder hope.
- A sorting process of expectations is required.
- We have the power to choose hope.

Some key scriptures to consider:

Proverbs 13:12; Ezekiel 37:11; John 14:16-17; Romans 4:18, 5:2-5; Hebrews 12:2; Romans 8:22-25; Deuteronomy 13:3

## LET'S CONNECT TO DISCUSS THIS CHAPTER:

**Join My Interactive Discussions:** Please come visit with me at www.IncreaseHope.com in section "Book Resources" where I will be posting specifically for this chapter. I invite you to leave your comments or questions and I'll personally be responding. I will also have audios and videos and other resources pertinent to the topics in this chapter.

**Join Our Live Events:** Carol and I also offer special events www.HopeAcceleratorSeminars.com for more personal and in-depth face to face training and equipping. I look forward to continued connection with you.

Blessings! - Arnold J. Allen

## *Personal Notes*

_____

_____

_____

_____

_____

_____

_____

_____

_____

_____

_____

_____

_____

_____

_____

_____

_____

_____

_____

_____

_____

_____

_____

_____

_____

As hope joins the grief process, the eternal, transcendent dimension of hope pulls grief beyond the present loss and into a promising future. Hope outlasts pain!

*Our hope for you is firmly grounded, knowing that you are sharers of our suffering, so also you are sharers of our comfort.*

II Corinthians 17 (NASB)

# 8
# Hope When it Hurts

## Outlasting Toxicity

Grief is powerful and loss is consuming. Hope and love, however, are greater. Without hope, grief and loss grow unchecked, creating a weight that pulls the heart into an overwhelming heaviness. With hope, love and time, grief and loss gradually lose their power.

Albert, a farmer friend of ours, lost his wife, Ethel, a number of years before we met him. As our friendship grew, we became a safe place for him to share his heart. We discovered that he was stuck in heavy loneliness since her death. Because of this, very little had changed in the farmhouse they once shared. Not surprisingly, little had changed in his life as well, as he carried out the duties of operating his small farm. Most conversations, especially those involving decisions about the homestead, ended with wondering what Ethel would have wanted. He was not free to move ahead without her. The grief and loss of her passing allowed a dark cloud to form over his heart and mind.

While he thought that he was honoring her, he was actually stuck in a place that she never would have wanted him to be.

In time and with the support of family and friends, Albert met another woman he could love. But even this was a difficult road. One of the big challenges for him, as is common for many, was to allow her into areas of his heart that had previously been reserved for Ethel. Eventually, hope and love released these locked up places to allow Albert to live again.

## The Grief Process

Grieving people require time to process. By design, we cannot just "snap out of it!" The greater the loss, the more involved the process of release. Through the recovery process, there are a number of spheres of experience that the grieving heart visits and revisits. Each sphere requires hope to manifest. When bound by grief, the heart cannot move on to new life-giving places. An emotional abscess develops, hidden until exposed as one revisits that sphere of loss. The revisit may come as a new, hurtful experience, or the remembrance of the situation. We can remain stuck in those places for a long time.

Dr. Bruce Thompson authored *Walls of My Heart* and founded the College of Counseling and Health Care for the University of the Nations. As a general practice, Dr. Thompson found that 80% of clients coming to him for medical care had illnesses that were not primarily biologically based. Rather, they had mental, emotional and spiritual issues manifesting as physical problems. Other researchers suggest the percentage may be as high as 95%! Treating the source of the problem was essential for effective, lasting relief—requiring change in the soul and spirit. Grief, coping with suffering and adjusting to loss are key elements in the wellness journey. Hope was a big part of that change.

Understanding the steps of the grief process, from inception to recovery, can be helpful in apprehending hope in the journey. Since there are many excellent resources to help in the grief process, I will only give a brief outline assembled from various sources.

- Initial Shock or Realization of Lost Expectation or Relationship
- Denial - Avoidance; Confusion; Fear; Numbness; Blame
- Anger - Frustration; Irritation; Anxiety; Embarrassment; Shame
- Questioning  - Why? Why not? If Only! Should Have/ Shouldn't Have!
- Depression - Overwhelmed; Helpless; Hostile; Flight; Blahs; Low Energy; Illness; Loneliness
- Bargaining - Struggle to Find Meaning; Reach Out to Others; Tell Story; Finding Hope
- Acceptance  - Exploring Options; New Plans; Moving On; Optimism; Renewed Purpose
- Return to Life or Forge a New Story - Empowerment; Security; Self-esteem; Meaning

## A Personal Process

Grief and loss may develop gradually as a situation erodes, or appear suddenly, as in cases of trauma. Obviously, all traumas are hurtful and chaotic. Abuse has a very wide range of intensity and severity. Because such experiences rarely fit into a neat process or sequence, it is difficult to identify our true condition while caught up in turmoil.

Depending on our personal makeup and the specific situation, one aspect or another of our being can experience greater pain at any given moment. Although completely interconnected, spirit, soul and body each have specific sensors to the trauma, abuse and loss. Consequently, the spirit will connect with certain aspects of experiences, the soul will engage other aspects and the body will feel it differently than either spirit or soul.

For some people, the battle is in their thoughts and emotions. Shock can create numbness and apathy as though there are no thoughts at all, only blank stares into nowhere. At other times, grief and loss flood the mind with racing monologues and incessant rehearsals of the traumatic situation. The content of this self-talk is usually related to the sphere of grief, especially in anger or questioning over the event. Since thoughts become manifest in emotions, these scripts enlarge and intensify the negative experience. Anger may flare for no apparent reason while the black hole of depression seems irreversible and bottomless.

Some situations of loss and trauma generate illness in physical feelings. Beyond the obvious trauma of an injury, individuals may experience pain in various body parts. Headaches, breathing problems, stomach problems, high blood pressure, skin issues or other physical symptoms may be sourced in grief, loss and trauma. At times, nerves feel raw and we avoid the greatly needed comfort of physical touch, conversely, we may medicate physical pain with drugs or sex. While the physical symptoms may be relieved somewhat through medication, lasting change requires addressing emotional, mental or spiritual issues manifesting in physical feelings. As we learned in Chapter 5, how we think influences our lifespan. Think negatively, die sooner. Think positively, live longer.

## The Toxicity of Grief

Our spirits have emotion, knowledge and experience that become expressed in the body and soul. The instinctive knowledge of the spirit flows into mental thoughts and physical feelings. Therefore, it is deeply affected by various losses and traumas. Sadness of spirit (1 Kings 21:5 NASB), anguish (Ex. 6:9 NKJV), a crushed and broken spirit (Proverbs 15:4, 18:14 NASB) are a few Biblical terms describing the spiritual response to trauma, grief and loss. As we have seen, the spirit also experiences a range of emotions. Impending calamity, anxiety, heaviness, a sense of uncleanness and confusion are some of the many emotions the spirit contributes.

As we encounter loss, our spirit, soul and body experience toxicity—a significant enemy of hope and wellness. Each aspect of our being experiences its own type of toxicity, and thus, requires a specific approach to address the poisonous residue.

There are various helpful cleansing programs available for the body. For example, a colonic or cellular cleanse, fasting or deep tissue massage are a few of many aspects of body cleansing. I will expand on this idea later in this book.

There are also processes to cleanse the soul and spirit, especially addressing toxic thoughts and emotions. Approaches that identify and remove false beliefs and skewed emotional and psychological patterns are helpful. Release from trauma

127

is essential. Healing of pain-filled memories and restoration of the wounded spirit are vital to hope renewal. When identified, deliverance from evil spirits is an essential cleanse. Mythical beliefs create specific spiritual toxicity. As we have seen from earlier chapters, memories and emotions are resident in the body and spirit as well as the soul. Reducing toxicity in the whole person increases hope flow, thus increasing health and quality of life.

## Hope Outlasts Pain

It is clear from scripture that God, by nature, is hope. The Spirit has innate hope. Therefore, as living beings, our hope source is dependent upon the Spirit of Life. The scripture says, "Anyone who is among the living has hope." (Ecc. 9:4 NIV) Simply because we are among the living, God's fullness becomes available to us. The Spirit is filled to overflowing with healing, comfort, deliverance, provision, support, joy and love. As the Spirit communes with our spirit, these aspects flow into our being. We can access an ever increasing life-flow, thus an increased hope-flow from the Spirit into our whole person.

Grief, trauma and loss are temporal. They only last so long. Hope does not have a time restriction. Hope can wait. As hope joins the grief process, the eternal, transcendent dimension of hope pulls grief beyond the present loss and into a promising future. God has "put eternity in the hearts of men" as Ecclesiastes 3:11 states. Hope outlasts pain!

Many times as a pastor, I found it sufficient just to be with a grieving family. Often, there was nothing that could be said to relieve the weight of loss. I prayed for them, but silent

128

companionship were more healing and comforting than talk, even if it was talking to God.

## Hope Prevails

I will never forget one such occasion of grief. Carol and I were having our annual Christmas open house. It was a time to have church families into our home, a celebration of eating together and fellowship in the festive season. In the midst of the festivities, the doorbell rang. It was no surprise to greet my neighbor. I invited him in but he insisted that I step outside where he informed me that a church family had been in a fatal accident on the way to my home gathering. Grabbing my coat, I left immediately for the hospital.

In a tense, grief-filled waiting room, the story unfolded. The mom, a woman whom I had spent many hours with over the previous couple of years, was dead. As one who had overcome terminal cancer for over two years beyond her expected survival, she was one of my heroes of perseverance. I had prayed with her weekly in her home and at the church. Her eldest son, twenty-one at the time, was also dead. Another teenage son was in very critical condition. It was uncertain if he would pull through. Other children and family arrived. Hugs, tears, brief prayers were all a part of that long night. Mostly, my help was just in being there for them. My presence brought hope and comfort in the midst of overwhelming grief. Such presence is especially influential when we have experienced similar grief at some point in our lives.

The days that followed were difficult as Christmas day approached. Christmas would never be the same. Life

129

would never be the same. The teenager pulled through and recovered to carry on a pretty much normal life. The family and church community eventually created a new "normal." The eldest daughter took on some responsibility for younger siblings and eventually married. The husband remarried as well. Although it has been over four decades since that fateful night, the memories of the sustaining power of authentic hope stay with me today. Hope prevails.

## A Healing Presence in the Pain

The scripture presents a powerful and convincing picture that Jesus knows our grief and loss in a personal way.

> This High Priest of ours understands our weaknesses, for He faced all the same testings we do, yet He did not sin.

Hebrews 4:15 (NLT)

The power of grief can be such that it seems impossible to hear God's voice. In these times, hope and love release a sustaining power. Like me that night in the grief-filled hospital waiting room, hope does not know why the loss occurred. Hope does not know how long the grieving process will be. Hope only knows Who is in the process. Hope knows the presence of God, and that all healing comes from Him and leads to Him.

I recall another story of deep loss. My friend Judy Blakeney's nine-year-old daughter had become suddenly ill. The source of the illness was not immediately identified. When the discovery was finally made that the appendix was the problem, it had already burst a couple days prior. The situation was critical.

The operation went well. It seemed that the surgeons had saved her life. Then complications came. She began to fail rapidly. Within hours, her young life was gone from this earth.

I was arrested by the intensity of this story. Thoughts of my own children and grandchildren came to mind. How does someone walk out of such grief and loss? Judy shared that it was a very slow process over months for her to move from unbearable grief to some aspect of grief management. The Lord had given the family a strategy during this time. When the oppressive, dark cloud of grief and depression began to settle in, she and her family were to begin to talk about their daughter Sarah.

"Here is what He said to us," Judy recounted. "Remember that Sarah is now in a place of joy and happiness. Recall how she loved to pick flowers and that there is a limitless supply for her now. Renew your hope of being with her in the future." This Spirit-designed strategy dissolved the dark cloud. Over the months, more insight began to develop for Judy and her family. This dark cloud was not just the grief of loss of her daughter. It was a spiritual attack from the enemy of her soul to weigh her down with despair. It was not just her grief. This dark cloud was made up of evil spiritual powers set on destroying her, the family and their ministry. The exposure of the enemy's strategy enabled Judy to overcome it more effectively.

The apostle Paul knew the tension of grief and hope. He expressed the deepest of grief over the refusal of his people to receive Jesus as the Messiah. "I have great sorrow and continual grief in my heart" (Romans 9:2 NKJV). He knew grief. He also knew hope. In fact, Paul wrote the most about hope of any of the New Testament writers. "Be joyful in hope, patient in affliction, faithful in prayer" (Romans 12:12 NIV). Hope provided a significant source of energy for perseverance for Paul (Romans 5). Hope flourishes even in the garden of grief.

## Hope Carries the Pain

Hope can exist in pain. It has to, for hope actually has power to reduce pain. A sustaining energy comes from the presence of hope. The inability to effectively process pain in life inevitably produces some degree of fatigue and reduces hope. Pain consumes energy. Hope restores energy.

Many of life's experiences produce pain in the heart. Because of this, no one lives completely apart from pain and suffering. These companions are common for many areas of our life experience, and are inescapable to some degree. Yet, they do not negate the work of hope. Indeed, it is in such difficult situations that the expression of hope is magnified.

Even God knows deep loss through the incomprehensible level of suffering that Jesus endured for our comfort, healing and hope. The Message Bible translates parts of Isaiah fifty-three and four like this:

> At first everyone was appalled. He didn't even look human – a ruined face, disfigured past recognition…. a man who suffered, who knew pain first hand. One look at him and people turned away. But the fact is, it was our pains he carried – our disfigurements, all the things wrong with us.

## Hope: The Covering Sanctuary

Pain without comfort, loss without sanctuary, grief without consolation—all can evolve into crippling despair. Hope is the key. Hope is the primary door to the place of comfort. Hope creates the place for sanctuary in times of loss. Knowing that a future exists without grief, ministers the consolation of hope. As the essence of hope, God manifests His character through transforming trouble and discouragement into purpose and future. God speaks gently to His people through the prophet Hosea. "I will give her... the Valley of Achor as a door of hope, she shall sing there, as in the days of her youth" (2:15 NKJV). *Achor* means trouble. It was the valley where Achan was stoned after sinning against God. His sin caused the army to be defeated in the first battle for the city of Ai. Fortunately, the desert of trouble and loss became a place of hope and rejoicing through God's help, as true today as it was then.

Pastor David Crone describes an insight from his journey of hope. He felt the Lord say:

> *Every loss and failure is the fertilizer that will give nutrition to the soil of your next harvest. They are either the septic poison that will kill your future, or they will be the nutrients for your future prosperity. The key to which one it will be is your response to failure and loss in light of who I am and what I have promised.*

> [David's response] God cannot allow any of the things we go through to go to waste. He always makes them to be for the benefit of those who

walk and co-labor with Him for the working out of His will in all these things.

So then, every loss, failure, success, hurt, joy, relationship, pain, sorrow, experience, circumstance—everything must work for my good. All of life can be made only to serve my advancement and the establishment of my destiny. Everything must bow to my destiny. Everything must bow to my good. My progress is not prisoner to my circumstance but my loss and failure are servants to my destiny.

People experiencing trouble, tests, grief, loss and suffering require hope for their survival. The voice of hope speaks truth through the heart, proclaiming a future beyond the pain. While grief and loss feel like the world is collapsing, hope draws us toward a more open posture. The situation may be difficult and painful, but the hopeful person remains expectant to possibilities. Hope survives. Hope flourishes.

## Shame: Hope's Wet Blanket

*But we have renounced the hidden things of shame…*

II Corinthians 4:2 (NKJV)

I watched an interesting interview recently. The guest, Brené Brown, is a popular writer and public speaker specializing in shame and vulnerability. In response to an audience question concerning how to handle criticism or being shamefully put down, she responded in a practical way. Grabbing her wallet, she pulled out a very small piece of paper, about an inch square. She explained that this paper contained the list of people from whom she was open to receive criticism. She went on to discuss other aspects of her experience but I could not help thinking about that little paper list. As I thought of creating my own list, I realized that the most powerful voice needed to be those closest to me. First on the list, for me, needs to be the Spirit. All other opinions fall under that.

Often, we are our own biggest critic, first on the list. It is our own self talk, our own measuring stick that endeavors to cast the disqualifying vote against making the cut. This is the voice of shame. For the most part, shame is crystallized in a key statement or question. "You are not good enough!" and "Who do you think you are?" While there are many variations of this challenge, the goal is the same. Restrict or stop forward movement! When the voice of the past is the primary contributor in relationships and decisions, we know our focus is on the rearview mirror rather than the window of future.

When it comes to relationships, shame will always draw fear, rejection, disappointment and false guilt to the horizon. True guilt, the awareness of having done wrong, is the fallout of bad choices, bad actions. These can be forgiven and become the fodder of good choices and actions. Guilt, properly handled, should have a positive outcome in relationship. False guilt, on the other hand, has no possibility of positive application. It is based on false information, a lie. Shame and false guilt partner in weaving the cloak of unworthiness and singing a dirge to our inner being.

Shame nearly always results in negative outcome. False guilt leads to shameful condemnation that attaches to our very being: "I am bad. If I was good, I wouldn't be blamed for being bad. Bad people aren't worthy of good things." This is fueled by accusations such as:

"You are always a rotten loser."

"You are not...."

"You never...."

We fill in the blanks: never pretty enough, never good enough, not talented enough, not powerful enough, not smart enough! As we move into a developing relationship, a business opportunity or some specific goal, authentic hope must contend with the voice of shame.

Obviously, we need both the rear view and the future view. However, the central focus in grasping the unfolding future cannot be the rear view. The rear view message of condemnation, accusation or shame is an assault on authentic hope. Energy, designed to possess the unfolding future, becomes consumed in the black hole of shame. The "warm wash of shame" is Brené Brown's expression in her popular TED Talk on shame. She is likely referring to the flush of embarrassment that we tend to experience with shame. I think of the feelings Adam must have had when God asked him: *"Who told you that you were naked?"* (Genesis 3). Obviously, God is not the source of shame, condemnation or accusation. Adam experienced shame before his conversation with God about his nakedness. The consequence of the "warm wash" is energy consumption. Feeling more like a wet blanket, it drains the energy from the very core of our being through a powerful rear view and a darkened future view.

## Pro-descending Father's Love

Recently while having coffee and recounting her Father's Heart Discipleship School experience with YWAM New Zealand, my friend Cindy made a very powerful statement. "Everything in our school was positioned and taught from the Father's love perspective. Condescending love cascaded into our lives. We experienced being loved by the Father. It was an experience based and Biblical based training to know God's love so deep that we were changed." I was surprised by the terminology. Due to the currently negative definition of condescending and my love of words, I began to make mental adjustments. How about descending love? Or to make it more positive: pro-descending love. She had my full attention. The bottom line goal of the school was to bring each student into an unforgettable revelation experience of being loved by Father God. Experiencing the cascading love of a passionate Father is more than enough antidote to the wet blanket or warm wash of shame. Once experienced, we can revisit cascading love when needed and desired.

In a significant, intrinsic way, shame and fear have become connected to nakedness. Adam and Eve were initially naked and unashamed (Genesis 2). Their nakedness was unapologetic and as natural to them as a little child. They were completely comfortable with their naked walks with God and each other in the garden. There was no warm wash of shame for them or God. No wet blanket to the open, trusting relationship. A very bad choice brought them into a spiritual, relational dimension that produced shame and fear in their relationship with each other and God. Along with many other consequences, the warm wash of shame established a foothold in humankind's relationship. With few exceptions, we are all aware of that nakedness/shame connection.

It seems obvious that shame-related nakedness is not just physical but also experienced in spirit and soul. The very core of our whole person is impacted by the powerful, pervasive influence of shame. Thus the covering for nakedness must be sufficient for the inner man of soul/spirit as well as the outer man of body.

For Adam, God covered his body with skins and devised a plan to cover the inner man and free humankind from shame. The initial step toward the exchange of hope for shame was doubt. We find it in the serpent's challenge in Genesis 3. Basically, "Did God really say....?" Thus a primary step out of shame is exchanging doubt for the restoration of hope. The primary antidote to the warm wash of shame is the cascading love-filled, life-giving, authentic hope.

In leaving behind the nakedness/shame connection, we can come to know the nakedness/hope connection. As with Adam, we will continue to be covered physically. We also have a covering through Christ for the inner man. There are many scriptures that describe this freedom from shame. The apostle Paul describes a powerful trinity in Philippians. He had been describing the Gospel being preached while he was in prison. Here he speaks of his own deliverance.

*I will rejoice for I know this will turn out for my deliverance through your prayers and the provision of the Spirit of Jesus Christ, according to my earnest expectation and hope, that I will not be put to shame in anything, but that with all boldness, Christ will even now, as always, be exalted in my body whether by life or in death*

Philippians 1:18-20 NASB)

His list includes the prayers of the Philippian believers, provision or supply of the Spirit and joining these with his hope. Rather than the "warm wash of shame" in his prison cell, Paul is counting on being awash in prayer, the Spirit and hope.

The apostle John writes so clearly he could well have been thinking about Adam when he wrote.

*Now, little children, abide in Him, so that when He appears, we may have confidence and not shrink away from Him in shame at His coming.*

I John 2:28 (NASB)

When Jesus wants time with us, we can experience expectancy and anticipation of being with Him. Even more powerful are the encouraging words of Jesus that John recorded in Revelation.

*You do not know that you are wretched and miserable and poor and blind and naked, I advise you to buy from Me gold refined by fire so that you may become rich, and white garments so that you*

> *may clothe yourself, and that the shame of your*
> *nakedness will not be revealed; and eye salve to*
> *anoint your eyes so that you may see.*

> Revelation 3:17-18 (NASB)

His glory covers our shame. Hope flourishes in His glory.

## Naked Hope

I am reminded of an amazing conversation with a woman with a revelation of the nakedness/hope connection. She worked for a while as a stripper. After coming to know the transforming love of Jesus, she began to experience a deep life transition. She described the long journey to become comfortable with herself in the nude. The shame associated with her nude body was nearly overwhelming. Nothing touches the depth of the soul and spirit quite like the shame of sexual abuse. As God brought healing and restoration to her, she was able to have love and respect while seeing her naked body in the mirror. Tears rolled down her cheeks as she shared the most intimate victory. In her private worship, she was able to dance naked and unashamed before her Creator. She had discovered what Eve must have experienced before her shame-generating choice. God's glory covered her shame! The cascading love of Father God empowered authentic hope to flourish, naked.

To embrace hope is to embrace vulnerability. To embrace vulnerability is to walk into the future naked, expectant and unashamed. This is authentic, shameless hope. Trust, engagement, accountability, adaptability, creativity: all are born from authentic, wholehearted hope. To disempower the influence of shame, we need to rethink and redefine how we engage hope. Authentic hope is the foundation for the fullest of life experience.

## Summary

Some of the key aspects of the relationship between hope, pain, suffering, grief, loss and shame are these:

- Hope exists in pain, grief & loss.
- A sustaining energy comes from hope.
- Grief is a process and can get stuck.
- Grief is experienced in body, soul and spirit.
- Bad experiences require cleansing from toxicity.
- Hope is a powerful antidote to pain.
- Hope offers sanctuary from grief and loss.
- Shame is different than guilt & false guilt.
- Shame nearly always results in negative outcome.
- Shame and fear became connected to nakedness.
- The initial step toward the exchange of hope for shame was doubt.
- We can exchange nakedness/shame for the nakedness/ hope connection.

Some key scriptures to consider:

Genesis 2, 3; Exodus 6:9; I Kings 21:5; Proverbs 15:4, 18:14; Ecclesiastes 3:11, 9:4; Isaiah 40:30, 53 & 54; Hosea 2:15; Romans 5, 9:2, 12:12; II Corinthians 1:7, 4:2; Philippians 1:18-20; Hebrews 4:15; Rev. 3:17-18

**LET'S CONNECT TO DISCUSS THIS CHAPTER:**

**Join My Interactive Discussions:** Please come visit with me at www.IncreaseHope.com in section "Book Resources" where I will be posting specifically for this chapter. I invite you to leave your comments or questions and I'll personally be responding. I will also have audios and videos and other resources pertinent to the topics in this chapter.

**Join Our Live Events:** Carol and I also offer special events www.HopeAcceleratorSeminars.com for more personal and in-depth face to face training and equipping. I look forward to continued connection with you.

Blessings! - Arnold J. Allen

**Personal Notes**

_____

_____

_____

_____

_____

_____

_____

_____

_____

_____

_____

_____

_____

_____

_____

_____

_____

_____

_____

_____

_____

_____

_____

_____

_____

_____

_____

_____

When the strength of our minds, emotions and hearts is exhausted, we are carried by authentic, transcendent hope.

*For we do not want you to be ignorant, brethren, of the affliction we experienced in Asia, for we were so utterly, unbearably crushed that we despaired of life itself.*

II Corinthians 1:8 (RSV)

# 9
# Finding Erica

## Hope in the Storm

Authentic hope, similar to love, finds its most powerful expression in the extremes of life. In the midst of favor, success, and prosperity, hope abounds with energy, breaks open new vistas for faith and energizes the capacity to love. In the midst of overwhelming grief, loss, and disappointment, hope is the only available living energy, sustains even the smoldering hint of flame and supplies a thread of future.

Moving beyond the range of experiences covered in Chapter 8, hope shines in even greater difficulties. The purpose of this chapter is to illustrate the hope journey in the life's extreme situations. Each journey unfolds uniquely. The sustaining nature of authentic hope undergirds all of our life experience, even the very most difficult. Although your circumstances are different, the sustaining energy of hope transcends even the most difficult situations.

Not long ago, family friends experienced a very difficult season in which hope was tested to the maximum capacity. Henry's wife, Erica, disappeared. For nearly three months, Henry Schmidt, his family and hundreds of others searched for Erica. Eventually, her body was discovered in a brushy woods in her home community. She had ended her own life. I will describe hope as it relates to suicide and other significant issues in the next chapter. This chapter is focused on the difficult journey of the living while dealing with the loss. Chapter 9 laid the foundation for authentic hope in grief, loss pain and suffering. From that foundation, we will join Henry in his journey.

Carol and I were not able to be with the family so we stayed connected from a distance. As I read Henry's media postings, I was deeply impressed with the active power of hope that sustained him and his family over the months. The tension and struggle between finite hope and ultimate, infinite hope illustrate the transcendent nature of authentic hope.

> *Day 5: It has been wonderful to see how God has raised up both a spiritual + natural army to cover this entire area. Erica's heart has always been to see a united body of intercessors rise up in this city and beyond. Here it is happening, although I don't think she ever thought it would happen this way. We are encouraged + hope to have good news that Erica is safe + sound soon!*

By this time the Search And Rescue (SAR) had been mobilized to cover many roads, paths and trails in the area. An unprecedented response from the community has generated a lot of leads but no positive results.

*Day 7: The time is longer than I had ever imagined possible + I cry out for the necessary endurance.*

*Day 9: The sun has risen + it was difficult to get out of bed today, but a friend is staying with me + together we "walked this mountain" one step after another. About 3 weeks before this began, the Lord gave me the word, "Enduring." I had little idea what this meant, but I now realize it is strength for one more day than what I thought I could walk yesterday. We shall endure by His grace. "I can do all things through Christ who strengthens me."*

## Connected With Support

As our natural hope wanes, the support of the Lord and friends becomes increasingly needed. For most of us in crisis, this juncture is revisited repeatedly, daily, hourly and in the moment. Discovering what we really need can be very difficult. Some people find it nearly impossible to express deep feeling and let others into that inner world. For others, everything comes pouring out like a flood. Each of us will be different. The important element is to stay connected with support.

*Day 13: Today, the phone rang + the police were asking me to view a street video to verify whether it was Erica. It's only 12 seconds long, but right when the figure came on screen I knew in my heart it was her, I cried out + started to weep with joy! We saw her clothes + without a moment's hesitation, agreed they were indeed hers; her hair, her walk, the way she lifted her purse strap*

*over her shoulder: "I just wanted to reach out +*
*pull her in!" So close, and yet not home. But our*
*hearts have been encouraged + we're believing*
*for the next pieces to come together, yield the full*
*picture + see her safe soon!*

This and other accounts of seeing Erica were later dismissed due to errors. Our hearts and minds will naturally reach for anything of substance that may give promise of connection. While it is natural to grasp for encouragement, the critical connection must be with the Lord through the Spirit. Otherwise, we will become disillusioned. As I will describe more fully in the next chapter, our hope gravitates toward its focus even if it is a false focus. The character and nature of God are the foundation for secure focus in authentic hope.

## More Than I Can Bear

*Day 16: Light came in the night concerning my need*
*to "know" answers to Questions? Like: "Where is*
*Erica? Is she OK? When will she come back?" And*
*I heard the Holy Spirit admonish me that focusing*
*on these Qs? is like looking back. Now I need to*
*look again to my spiritual roots + draw from that*
*same Tree of Life - what I do know. Just over 4*
*years ago, Erica's life also hung in a balance. The*
*Lord spoke Job 23:10 (NJKV) to me, "He knows*
*the way that I take." And what do I know? He knew*
*my way + brought us through then + I know His*
*Presence. I know Erica is with Jesus. Whether still*
*with us here on earth or in heaven, I don't know; but*

*I do know He is faithful, He has never left us. He has not forsaken her, nor will He ever!*

*I recently read an article debunking nice religious-sounding phrases, well-meaning but lifeless clichés such as: "God never gives you more than you can handle." Sounds good, eh?*

*But I find myself now crying out, "This is more than I can handle!" But God has shown me: it's not about how much or how well I can handle. I am "hard pressed, but not crushed; struck down, but not destroyed." I cannot do or handle all things, let alone shoulder these things, this weight and burden of loss I feel. He alone "bears all things, believes all things, hopes all things, endures all things." The "Footprints" poem has taken on a whole new dimension of meaning for the Schmidt family.*

Henry makes an important point in this painful cry. We actually do have times that demand more of us than we have to give. Paul writes in II Corinthians, Chapter 1 (NKJV) about his trip to Asia. He describes it as "the sentence of death on ourselves." Again in 12:9, "My grace is sufficient for you, for My strength is made perfect in weakness." Just as Paul needed to hope on the One who "raises the dead," Henry is forced to the source of hope. When the strength of our mind, emotions and heart is exhausted, we are carried by authentic, transcendent hope.

## Pulling the Heart into Hope

*Day 30: Discouragement rears its ugly head. The*

*police have said the trail has gone cold. At times our trail/walk/journey here on earth seems to grow cold. Only bits of information, but the dots didn't connect. But it seems right now we don't even have any dots! So we must walk through this darkness, this absence of light, by faith. Faith trusts God: "the evidence of things not seen." Faith trusts the One who made the world out of nothing to bring sense out of no sense. When nature and its "facts" or lack of them say it's impossible, Our God: the God with whom all things are possible, speaks and acts! We may feel: DIS-couraged, DIS-tressed, our vision has DIS-appeared + we are DIS-appointed, but we cannot let the enemy "DIS" us. Let the Blood + Love of Jesus wash + break off the "DIS'es: We're not dis-qualified, but qualified, not dis-approved, but approved because He is ever faithful who has called us. His faith + love remove the "dis" from our temporary dis-appointments; so we are ready for His Appointment!*

Henry is not just doing some mental calisthenics here but allowing the truth to pull his heart into hope. Although he uses the word *faith*, he is actually describing the character of Biblical hope. Hope does not see the outcome, yet trusts. Hope does not know how things will turn out, yet depends.

The local police sponsored a media blitz in their home. The family put out a plea to the community for help available.

*We also got to tell Erica's story: how she's taken on being part of the solution for pain in our world today, helping bring healing in Africa to the UJV - Uganda Jesus Village: former orphan/victim/child soldiers from Kony's rebel army, but now sons + daughters in Christ's. In each of the last 4 years, she has spearheaded packing up to 15 suitcases of everything from underwear to school supplies for these needy kids. This year, she's already packed 3 suitcases for a trip we're planning for January. So, in the midst of our pain, the message came through, Jesus-followers have vision beyond bad news, despair, or even our self. The Gospel, the Good News of Jesus Christ, always turns prodigal hearts home to the Father's embrace!*

*Day 40: My daughter, Amy + I sat in our living room, our only light focused on The Prodigal Son picture still secure above the fireplace. Brian Doerksen's song "Will You Worship?" rose in my spirit, I answered "Yes!" + ran for refuge into those loving arms of the Father's embrace. Job lost everything he had in this world in the space of a few hours, yet he worshiped God. He did not serve God for mere things, his own prosperity, motives or ends.*

*Day 49: This is a Grand Canyon depth, an Everest height, like I'd never imagined possible. Indeed, without God this is impossible. At times I've felt abandoned, like the "Footprints" author. I then need to trust He is carrying me. Other times I've pleaded for Him to just give us at least a hint, some clue, any indication of Erica's whereabouts.*

*But the silence has seemed deafening. I've stood at our living room window, looked out into the darkness, believed for her to reappear, and conjured up all the faith I can in my heart to see her walk up the driveway. But I still stand there alone, waiting. 49 days is a long time. Sometimes I simply don't know what to do and waiting becomes not only enduring 1 day more, but merely the next hour or minute. Eternity seems turned upside down and inside out at the same time. My perspective is no longer the same. Trust is my only peace: a simple trust that Erica is with Jesus and He is true to His Word. He has never left nor forsaken her, nor ever will.*

*I must believe He is a loving God of His Word. It's Friday, but Sunday's coming! Our faith rests on this indisputable fact: Jesus rose from the dead! And Erica will too one day + so will all who put their faith in Jesus! I've been like those 2 disciples on their Luke 24 Journey to Emmaus. I know He is with us; I just don't see Jesus or Erica yet. I can identify with them: sad, confused, depressed, unaware this was the resurrected Jesus walking with them, opening up the prophetic Scriptures, causing their hearts to burn within.*

*Jesus indicated He would go farther; and again like them, my whole body, soul and spirit constrain Him to stay. He did and at the table, He took the bread, blessed, broke and gave it to them. "Then their eyes were opened…" just like Job's when he no longer only heard about God, but now saw Him! "And they knew Him." Oh, how I want to know Him, His ways, not just His Hand, but His face in new revelation! And so He leads + I will follow Him into Day-Step 50:*

## Until?

*Day 57: "How long, O Lord?!" The Psalms are filled with this recurring refrain. Not knowing is our natural human condition, but we also crave answers. God alone has the answers. Where + When? Where have we come from? Where is this all going? Where is Erica? How many times I've cried out, "It's too long already, Father! This is more than enough! It's unbearable! Can't You, won't You, bring this to some resolution/closure/conclusion already?" Then I hear myself like that impatient child in the back seat of the family van crying out, "Are we there yet?" I'm the child in the back seat and Abba Father is driving. And His answer to me is not merely, "Just a little while longer!" but in His Peace: "Until." My impatience replies, "Until? Until the 12th of Never? Will this go on forever? Is there no closure or resolution? Will we never know what has happened to Erica?" And my fear + frustration object: "This journey is no fun; this doesn't feel like a family holiday!" Yet He constantly assures me: "Until."*

*"Until the day breaks and the shadows flee away..."*
*Song of Songs 4:6*

*"Until these calamities have passed by..." Ps 57:1*
*in the shadow of your wings I will make my refuge.*

*"Until the time that his word came to pass...Ps*
*105:19 the word of the Lord tested him.*

*Until I went into the sanctuary of the Lord... Ps*
*73:16-17.*

*Until I know His Peace + Presence in my own*
*heart. Closure and resolution must come from*
*within, not dependent on good news from some*
*outside source.*

*Like the child in the back seat, I must learn to rest*
*and trust in the Lord: He is in control and He is*
*working even all these things together for good.*
*We are not headed into nothingness for never. I*
*cannot go to all the questions of what I do not know*
*about Erica's disappearance. But I can follow*
*Jesus, I not only can, but must.*

## Uganda Christmas Journey

*Day 70: Getting ready for Christmas just isn't the*
*same without her here with us. The outdoor lights*
*are up - she always wants lots of lights! A candle*
*burns in the window, literally and spiritually, a*
*hopeful beacon to guide her home. Our tree is up*
*too - it's gold + green this year: symbolic of what*

is pure, refined, precious, and filled with promises of hope + life. Our grandkids, Anya, Zander + Judah, hung the last few ornaments and crowned it with an angel whose electric wings fan the Spirit throughout the room!

And if you bend your ear close enough, you can hear many voices singing with her; "myriads of myriads, ten thousands of ten thousands and more thousands': "Glory to God in the highest and on earth peace to all men!" And my heart cries for peace this Christmas, for the Prince of Peace to rise. There's such great need for peace. And our home just feels empty without Erica: our Mom + Grandma + my wife.

But for now I wait, and hearken back to a Christmas just a few years past when God broke us out of our comfort zone and invited us on His journey to break open new horizons. Erica had tired of our traditional Canadian Christmas celebrations centered round just our own family. We'd always reached out to others in our community: invited those who had no family to join us for Christmas dinner. But Erica's heart hungered for more. Why not Christmas in Africa with Uganda Jesus Village, an orphanage of 63 victims of war, famine and disease?

Erica + I had been there two years before. Erica's heart desire to spend Christmas with these less fortunate began to take shape. Instead of looking *for presents under our tree, we would instead take some to those who had none. And the plan came together. Flights were confirmed, the money came in, tickets were purchased and Erica went on a shopping spree. Preparing for months, gathering clothing -she matched sizes for each from oldest to the youngest, Kevan, a little 6-year old girl suffering with AIDS. And school supplies - crayons, pens, pencils, note paper, books and food - snacks, treats, goodies that these children would have never otherwise seen. And lots of love.*

*We arrived in Uganda a week before Christmas and Erica went to work to see her dream fulfilled. We moved into Maria Prean's Guest-House. Celebrating Christmas properly had to include a dinner of course. Invitations now went out to all who had no place, no food, no family, no one to celebrate Christ's birth with. The guest list kept growing as we heard of more and more with no place to go.*

*Erica made multiple visits to the market for what our suitcases hadn't carried. And finally it was Christmas morning! And the Christmas story unfolded once again into reality. We returned home from church and, in true Ugandan fashion, the power went out just before the guests started arriving. But that couldn't stop about 25 crowding the dining hall: UJV staff, Mama Rose's children, Remi's 2 boys, Teacher Mike, Lorna, Peter,*

*Memory + 3 girls from the slums, Father's Heart choir, Stuart, Kira + their newborn Kaehler, their Australian friend, and 2 Austro-German ladies, visitors in the Guest House. They didn't want to intrude but, "No problem!" Erica countered, "There's room for you too!" They not only came, but even offered to buy the sodas for everyone! The multiplication was happening: all one BIG happy family! We couldn't fit everyone into Stuart + Kira's house, so Ann the Kenyan caretaker, opened up the Guest-House dining room and joined us too!*

*It was a truly Biblical banquet: the poor, fatherless, and widowed, those who were alone, without families, those were the ones Erica had always wanted for Christmas, and she got her wish. The chicken was a bit tough, the matoke a little bland to our Canadian taste, but there was beef, rice, potatoes, yams, and it was all good. There was more than enough, and whoever wanted went back for thirds. And not just for food, but warmth, love and Jesus showed up in our midst!*

*Then time for presents! Erica's suitcases disgorged more than they were naturally capable of carrying: a fire truck for one of Remi's sons. Erica had packed miraculously: just the right present for each one! She'd even found some embroidered towels for the German ladies! And as Ann, the caretaker guest in her own Guest-House, opened hers, tears started flowing down her cheeks. She confided this was the first Christmas present she'd ever received! And that made it all worthwhile!*

*Tears of emptiness, loneliness and sorrow: all turned to joy as our African Christmas bore its fruit. Christmas' true meaning had been rediscovered and we all went to sleep filled and fulfilled, happy to have been part of this ongoing miracle of Christ's birth where He is born again in hearts that have made room for Him.*

*And so, this Christmas, barring an expected miracle, there will be an empty seat at our dinner table. But I choose to look to + remember the many chairs and hearts Erica filled at times like that Christmas in UJV and led us to experience Christ, the true meaning of Christmas and beyond.*

As Henry recalls Erica and her passions, hope is renewed. Strength, energy to keep living, capacity to celebrate and create memories with the family, hope has its subtle movement ahead in the loss. There were many beautiful and wonderful ways that Erica expressed her passion. In many ways, she had invested her life into others, especially the less fortunate. Sometimes we get stuck in a moment in time, frozen in the loss, numb to the fuller reality of life.

## Hope Toward Closure

On Day 88, January 1, the police met with Henry and the family. Erica's body was found in nearby bushes. An area that had been searched various times without success yielded its hidden secret.

It's been 2 weeks since our Tribute service and the Lord is walking us through this continuing portion of our journey. One day at a time. Enduring one day more than I thought I could yesterday. But peace and confidence are now replacing the confusion which threatened to engulf us for so long. What was an emptying tiredness has turned into filling. My family + I now sense His healing Presence and growing strength in us.

Thank you for your notes, phone calls, cards— cards were always Erica's love-language and she would be amazed at the pile still growing in our family room. We sent over $2000 with Pastor Larry to Uganda this week + he is using these donations to fund Special Projects with the Uganda Jesus Village Kids Camp.

[A year later] Last New Year's Eve, about twilight, I heard sirens wail. Little did I know, a few doors down, another man, intoxicated, running from the police + God, heard those same sirens + ran in the opposite direction... down the hill, around a gas station, behind the car wash, slipped down an embankment, right into a maze of blackberries. Confused and frightened, rather than run out, he then ran further in + stumbled across Erica's body.

We had searched for 88 days, actually put up our 1st Missing poster at that very station. Search + Rescue had passed within a few feet of her. From the experience, that man's life changed and he has *been in rehab since! Much yet remains a mystery to me…Our God is a Redeemer: the only One I know who can take what the enemy intended for evil and somehow by His Grace work it for good. This year He has walked me and our family through the pain, confusion and loss of our dear Erica. We miss her greatly, but His Presence is with us, healing our hearts + turning her legacy for good.*

*[Another three months later] Friends ask, "How are you doing?" And depending on my day, I've sometimes dejectedly responded (and maybe you too?), "I'm going through it!" The last 3 weeks I've been "going through it': sorting, sifting, down-sizing through 35 years of marriage memories, but I've come to this realization: "Going through it" does not mean: starting well but getting so bogged down I become stuck in life's details; giving up on dreams; or losing hope that I'll ever apprehend that for which I've been apprehended.*

*One day Jesus told his disciples to get in the boat and He'd join them on the other side. He did not tell them about the adversities they'd meet half-way through. Neither did He tell them He'd also be giving practical lessons on walking on water through storm-tossed seas. But He did. And these men of little faith grew. One even got out of the boat and walked through the wind and waves, the storm and fears, the doubts and confusion. Sure, Peter started sinking when he changed his focus from Jesus to his problem, and so have I. But when Jesus says, "I am with you always" He's as good as His Word + He's been here with me + for me - all the way through. And this revelation yields comfort, peace and even joy!*

*Today is moving day and "I AM coming through it!" The "other side" still waits in the distance: But, I see the home shore coming ever closer and clearer. Whatever you're facing, remember: By God's grace, "You'll get through it!'*

## Centering Power of Ultimate Hope

Henry completed his move into a new home with his daughter's family. He has also returned to his mission endeavors, bringing an eternal life message to many in foreign lands. With trips to Mexico, Nepal, Uganda, Ghana, Nigeria and various other nations, he has been able to experience a renewed hope, prospering relationships and a new level of support for others in the journey of life.

Some critical points of development were key to sustaining Henry and his family. They experienced an amazing community support. This required an openness of the family to connect with others. For many years, they invested their lives into the community. The return was not only among friends but many hundreds of others joined in support. We may not find the level of support that we need in difficult times but we can always give support to others. The act of giving is, in itself, hope-building and provides a sense of meaning in the face of the nonsense of loss.

Finite hope that Erica would return ran along side the openness to receive infinite hope from God in the darkest hours. Henry was able to regularly and continually turn his focus back to the sustaining power of God when there was no other place to turn. Finite hope always has its limits, its boundary. It is essential to pursue the centering power of ultimate hope when everything in our world feels dead. When the only thread to hang on to is God, hanging on will ultimately bring change. "You'll get through it!"

## Summary

Some key aspects of hope from Henry's journey:

- Sustaining nature of authentic hope undergirds all of our life experience.
- As our natural hope wanes, the support of the Lord and friends becomes increasingly needed.
- We actually do have times that demand more of us than we have to give.
- When strength is exhausted, we are carried by authentic, transcendent hope.
- Truth pulls the heart into hope.
- Hope does not know how things will turn out, yet depends.
- Hope believes He is a loving God of His Word.
- In recalling memories and passions, hope is renewed.
- Hope is enduring one day more than I thought I could yesterday.
- Hope walks us through the pain, confusion and loss
- Finite hope always has its limits.

Scriptures used or referred to:

Job 23:10; Psalms 57:1, 73:16-17, 105:19; Song of Solomon 4:6; Luke 24; John 6:19; II Corinthians 1:8, 12:9; Philippians 4:13

## LET'S CONNECT TO DISCUSS THIS CHAPTER:

**Join My Interactive Discussions:** Please come visit with me at www.IncreaseHope.com in section "Book Resources" where I will be posting specifically for this chapter. I invite you to leave your comments or questions and I'll personally be responding. I will also have audios and videos and other resources pertinent to the topics in this chapter.

**Join Our Live Events:** Carol and I also offer special events www.HopeAcceleratorSeminars.com for more personal and in-depth face to face training and equipping. I look forward to continued connection with you.

Blessings! - Arnold J. Allen

*Personal Notes*

_____

_____

_____

_____

_____

_____

_____

_____

_____

_____

The neural pathways in the brain, physical appetites, the flow of thoughts and spiritual energy connected to authentic hope become networked to an alternate focus.

*Since the sun nor stars appeared for many days, and no small storm was assailing us, from then on, all hope of being saved was gradually abandoned.*

Acts 27:20 (NASB)

# 10
# Hope Hijacked

## Navigating the Focus of Hope

Walking through the New York airport enroute to a connecting flight with his children on September 11, 2001, my son-in-law Tim pointed out the Twin Towers of the World Trade center. Within the hour, the buildings were in flames, their flight cancelled. On 9/11, the hijacked airliners became weapons of destruction. Airliners which, through a complex network of systems and design, were intended to serve people, became tools of death and destruction. Not only did the passengers and building occupants perish, but millions of lives were altered forever.

As horrific as this memory is, however, please journey with me into a metaphor of hope.

By design, airliners fulfill the desires, dreams and ambitions of owners, pilots and passengers. Whether for business, family functions or recreation, each flight has a specific goal and planned route. Although packed with an enormous diversity of people and goods, all airliners depart and arrive at specific locations. The over-arching agenda of the airline industry is to serve the individual agendas of the passengers. On September 11, 2001, all of the flights in the entire industry lifted off the ground with the same purpose and goal. Tragically, four of those flights were hijacked for another agenda.

By design, each human being has a life empowered with hope-filled desires, dreams and ambitions. Packed with an enormous diversity of gifts, talents and resources, the over-arching intention in life is to experience the fulfillment of this innate potential through relationship. Although every life is conceived with the same purpose, many lives get hijacked every day for another agenda—one of bondage, destruction and death.

Like the airliners on 9/11, hope can be hijacked—anxiety, addictions, trauma and suicide being four of the most powerful, pervasive violators. They work by skewing our focus, affecting the basic elements of hope: our expectation, anticipation and belief. Abandoning the promise of an authentic, hope-filled life, our energies become harnessed to an agenda of destruction—an alternate destination.

Just as an airliner relies on a GPS to stay on course, authentic hope navigates by focusing on intention, engaging its resources to arrive at the destination. Negative forces can sabotage ultimate hope like the terrorist taking over the controls of an airliner. Unfortunately, when hope is hijacked and its navigation altered, its amazing power pulls toward an alternate destination, one that often ends in flames.

As I explained with the placebo response, the synergy of the hope energy is powerful. The Creator's original intention is that the hope destination be filled with promise and life. Hope, by design, moves toward a given destination. In the hands of a hijacker, it moves a person toward bondage, destruction and death, causing an internal tension between hijacked hope and life-oriented hope. A dark shroud cloaks the hope flame. The hijacked thoughts and feelings focus on bondage, destruction and death. Yet the original, innate hope continues to wrestle toward freedom, liberty and survival. Hope will maintain its powerful effort to survive until its last breath, its last thought, its last communion.

## Transference of Power

The hijacker endeavors to shift the power of a promising future to a constricted perspective where there seems to be no choice, no belonging, no future, and no authentic hope. With the sense that one's world is collapsing in on itself, why hang on for one more day? The ever-present pain is simply too much to live through. The hijacker uses false comfort to medicate and mask the pain. Anger, drugs, alcohol, sex and suicidal thoughts become part of the "better place" illusion suggested by the intruder. In the moment, there seems to be no other option, no better choice about the future.

Endeavoring to tilt the scales, dark spiritual powers become attached to the struggle. The hijacker's hand is strengthened as physical energy is depleted, emotions become heavy and thought patterns revisit dark destinations. File drawers of positive, life-giving heart memories are hacked and inaccessible as if they never existed. Files of fear, failure, shame and rejection are displayed on the table of the mind, easily accessed for repeated visits. The sense of personal pain is elevated. Like uncontrollable tremors of an earthquake, the very core of our being is captured and traumatized by these greater powers. While we put on a happy face for family, friends or co-workers, the real focus is on the dark hole of escape. Somehow, the pain must end. Dark spirits join our hopelessness in presenting a solution, albeit a placebo, instead of a life-giving, promise-filled future.

How have the hijackers gained access to hope—the central power supply of future? Traumas of war, rape, rejection, treachery and abuse are among the many agents of betrayal, handing the controls of the future over to hijackers. Whether by a single traumatic event or through erosion over years of perpetual assault, the neural pathways in the brain, physical appetites, the flow of thoughts and spiritual energy connected to authentic hope become networked to an alternate focus.

Pain demands a response. It must be answered, quenched or at least mitigated. How one responds to pain determines the future. The focus of hope, the synergy of hope energy, and the future story of the soul determine how we respond to pain. Hijacked hope has a dismal focus, a misguided energy, a dark future story. Fortunately, it is not the only future story.

## The Basis of Hope

A brief review of the nature and function of hope will refresh our understanding of the difference between an authentic and skewed future story. The biology of hope describes the physical aspect of hope. The body, including the brain and major organs, has memories and emotions from the past experiences and includes future-oriented energy. The brain is part of the storage system using chemical and electrical activity to encrypt, store and retrieve information and experiences. The heart mysteriously stores the detailed record of life experience and is a significant influence on the future story. The physical may be considered the hardware of memory.

I have suggested that the mind, with its connection to emotion, is primary in the psychology of hope. Thought patterns, mental attitudes, ideas of control and autonomy, and ways that we deal with life are aspects of psychology. The things that we think about, the focus of our perception of the future, and how we respond to memories are primary influencers in one's future story. The mind may be considered the software of memory. The mind relies on the brain—the hardware—to provide necessary neuro-pathways and various chemicals in the formation, storage and retrieval of thoughts and emotion. Researchers use the adage: "What fires together, wires together." Simply put, thoughts and emotions create a neuro-pathway to a memory— good or bad. When we have an experience similar to a past event, the brain plugs the mind into a neuro-pathway and its associated memory. For example, at the unexpected sound of an exploding firecracker, a war veteran may find himself in a battlefield memory. Or the fragrance of a perfume may invoke childhood memories of grandma's story-time readings. The physical touch of someone may bring comfort or painful response associated with past abuse.

The spiritual aspect of human nature will experience,

evaluate and store information from another dimension. This information, gathered by intuition, premonition and conscience, is integrated into the physical and mental memory. Not limited to time or distance, the spirit gathers insight from people and situations in the past and current relationship journey. This is because individuals tend to be influenced specifically by the spiritual condition of those they interact with. Whether aware of it or not, people at a party, at work or in sexual contact, for example, are in spiritual communication with one another. Drugs, alcohol, sexual arousal or illegitimate spiritual activity have a similar affect; they put the spirit, mind and body into an altered state. Trauma, sex, pain, addiction, suicidal thoughts and abuse always have a spiritual dimension. On the positive side, worship, prayer, legitimate sex, comfort, and life-giving future thoughts also have a spiritual dimension. Spiritual powers, either benevolent or malevolent, are influencers of the personal, human spirit. We are spiritual beings.

## Integrated Hope

The spirit, soul and body are completely integrated so that activity in any area clearly influences the whole. Any separation of these is solely for the purpose of discussion and understanding. Practically speaking, most hijackings of individual hope come from many small choices as the mind begins to focus on a specific course of action. The first illicit sex act, drug or alcohol use may be recreational or to medicate pain. With repeated illegitimate activity, however, the brain is altered, emotions prostituted and the spirit dulled. Over time, physical desires, emotional pain or spiritual vulnerability demand more relief, so more false comfort is sought. A point comes where the relationship with the hijacker has the upper hand most of the time. Eventually, a portion of the basic elements of hope—expectation, anticipation and belief—become submitted to the hijacker.

Trauma is a unique contributor to this decline. Much like the terrorist commandeering an airliner, another power takes authority through trauma. Unless self-inflicted, trauma comes from an act or event done to us rather than the process of taking over from within. While nearly all bondage seems like it is not within one's control, trauma tends to feel like another power has hacked in and captured the ability to respond. It bypasses choice while flooding the person with thoughts, feelings and unmanageable energy, triggering a reaction. It may feel like the reaction is automatic, unchosen. Trauma often carries elements of disguise and surprise, creating a perpetual vigilance for the hijacker's unannounced arrival.

An important aspect of understanding the brain's role in hope, addiction, dissociation or suicidal thoughts is the relationship of neuro-pathways and endorphins—the feel good brain chemicals. Similar to a dose of morphine, just thinking about relief of pain releases certain chemicals that actually reduce pain sensation. We know that hope has been hijacked when the thoughts of relieving pain illegitimately feel better than thoughts of living in present reality.

Repeatedly submitting oneself to an illegitimate source of comfort or pain-relief creates addiction. As I said earlier, pain demands a response. However, God's way is the re-orientation of thoughts toward authentic hope— a redemptive, life-generating pathway toward true comfort, companionship and relief. As the brain releases the endorphins connected to hope, pain subsides and the heart gets connected to future.

## Freedom Found: Harold's Hope Journey

There are ways to experience a renewed heart and mind. I will describe additional ways to cleanse, create and nurture hope in the next chapters. To close out this chapter, my friend, Harold Eberle, describes his own personal journey and the strategy he used in the pursuit of freedom from hopelessness and pain. Here is an excerpt from him speaking about his journey into freedom:

> For 11 years, my greatest personal struggle was depression. I'd have 3 days a week where all that I could think about was all of the stupid things that I've ever done. At least 2 days a month, I had suicidal thoughts during which I just tried to stay alive. As a hunter, I had guns in the house and often thought that I just wanted to end it all.
>
> Then while on a ministry trip in Toronto Canada, a psychiatrist came to me after a meeting and said, "You are a mess! You get so hyped up, I bet you have 2 or 3 days of depression after you preach. You must exhaust every chemical in your brain. You use up all the chemicals so you can't have a positive thought again." He was right.
>
> Now, the things that went through my mind were not what others would think were a big deal. They were the stupid things, and unfortunately, I have

done a lot of stupid things.

Everyone instantly files memories in certain places in our brain. Thoughts are filed at the depth of importance, depending upon how long you want to remember them. It's a sub-conscience thing. Memory is more than short-term and long-term. It is stored on an entire spectrum of time. We decide when we want to remember it. Whether it is one minute or 3 weeks or a year or 10 years, your brain instantly puts a value on the memory. If you don't care about information, you forget it.

Every place that you file a thought, there are neurons shaped like your hand and cells with dendrites sticking out. Then there are other neurons and little sparks and chemicals going across between them. Every thought has neurons that sustain it within the brain. We have 2 billion of these little things in our brain. Every thought that we have is programmed this way right now. Coincidentally, it is possible to physically burn a spot in the brain and the memory disappears. Everything that we think, exits in the neurons. It is physically in our brains.

So every time that we get new information, our brain decides where it is planted. My brain kept track of every stupid thing that I had ever done. Memory is stored at the depth of their importance. We tend to value things in areas of our life where we hold our self to high expectations. I excelled in science and math. To explain how irrational my thoughts were, in 7th grade, I missed 2 questions on a science test. I beat myself up for missing one of those questions until I was 41 years old. Irrational! That makes no sense! Every few days, that same stupid question would come to the surface and I would say: "I'm an idiot!!" I would repeat "I'm an idiot," because I learned through the years that when I said this, the thought would recede. But if I didn't say: "I am an idiot," then the thought would continue to bug me. How idiotic is that?

As part of my recovery, I learned that the brain is constantly reforming. It is plastic and every cell has to reproduce itself. Every 7 years, every cell in the body will be replaced with new cells. Several hundred thousand cells are replaced every day. Our brains are continually asking us if we want to hold a memory or not. There are a certain set of memories that we are saying, "I want this memory." Every few days, memories come to the surface, the forefront. We don't even realize that we are deciding: "Hold that memory or get rid of that memory." The brain is merely asking if the memory is important or not. We don't decide to keep it, only whether it is important or not.

Typically, I did not have old thoughts come to the surface if I was very busy. Book writing, phone calls, listening to people, playing with pets, and I'd be fine. But as soon as I was not busy, those thoughts came. As soon as I was alone and quiet, those old thoughts would return. I didn't understand that then but I do now. There was a certain set of memories that were right there. Memories that I thought were important. The questions that I missed were important and ready to surface.

Each person has their own memories that bug them. We make a mistake raising kids? We say, "I will never do that again! That was so stupid!" We may hold ourselves to a high standard on money. We may say to ourselves, "I will never do that again" as soon as we realize a bad investment.

As a public speaker, communicating precisely is important to me. Of course, being human, every time I speak, I say at least two stupid things. Considering how much I speak in a year, that is a lot of stupid things that I have said. In quiet moments, I will question myself: "Why did I say it that way?" When we hold ourselves to a high standard, we remember mistakes and say: "I will never do that again!"

The brain attaches emotion to the important, deep memories. In one part of the brain, there are two areas called the amygdala. When we have a really important memory, they go: SQUIRT! There is a release of chemicals that attach an emotion to the memory. The emotion that was attached to my stupid memories was shame. "WHY DID I MISS THAT QUESTION?!" It was in 7th grade, for crying out loud! It was stupid and irrational to blame myself, but that was my irrational thinking.

So here I was from 30 to 41 years old with a constant flow of these irrational thoughts. Sometimes they would come while asleep. Our mind continues to get things done in our sleep. I came to understand that when the memory came to the surface, my brain was asking if I should keep the thought or get rid of it. If I said, "I am an idiot," the thought would recede. When it came to the surface, a shock of shameful emotion would come with it. Four days later, the thought would return along with the feeling of shame. I was living in torment.

In Matthew Chapter 18, Jesus is asked by Peter how many times must we forgive another's faults. In response, Jesus tells a parable to explain forgiveness. It is like a king...... If you don't forgive your debtors, you are tortured. Interestingly, I had no problem forgiving other people, but I couldn't forgive myself. I was tortured for 11 years for not forgiving myself. My own mind was continually bombarding me with shame. Stupid things were tormenting me and I couldn't get rid of them.

In 1 John 1:7-9 we read: "If you confess your sins, He is faithful and righteous to forgive and cleanse." I understood forgiveness but not cleansing. Then I realized that confess meant to "agree with." If I agree with God like this verse says, He will forgive AND cleanse. Unfortunately, I was agreeing with shame but not with God! When that 7th grade question would come to mind, I agreed with the memory that it was a stupid mistake, not with God! When I would say: "I'm an idiot," I was not forgiving myself and not being cleansed. My mind held the memory and four days later it would be back. I was agreeing with the thought, experiencing the shame, and so it wasn't forgiven by me. But if I agreed with God, He would forgive me. The King in Jesus' parable could forgive 10 million dollars, yet I wouldn't forgive 10 dollars! I thought I had no right to forgive myself. But God forgives me of everything! I finally realized that it is stupid to hold this against myself. If I agree with God about these things, He not only forgives me but also cleanses me. Praise God!

## I Forgive Me

When we forgive ourselves (by accepting God's forgiveness), neurons actually detach from the memory. I learned that if I would focus for four days on forgiving myself, I would experience the cleansing that I so desired. I determined to do it. These memories were attached to emotion. To change my way of remembering, I needed to forgive myself with enough emotion to activate the amygdala into releasing chemicals with the positive emotion. I wanted it activated with thoughts of acceptance rather than thoughts of shame.

My psychiatrist taught me to see myself from

outside myself. When the negative thoughts came, I would confess: "I forgive you Harold!" The more emotion that I could put into the confession, the greater the impact on my brain. "I forgive you!" In my walking around, everyday life, I would speak out loud, "I FORGIVE YOU!!" Every time the old thoughts came, I would confess self-forgiveness and accept God's forgiveness, not just pretend. The deeper-seated memories required confession with powerful emotions of warmth, love and acceptance.

It worked. Within four days, I got rid of more than 90% of the negative memories. The remainder of the month, I worked on the rest of them. I don't even remember the old thoughts any more. I became a healthy human being in my thinking.

Forgiveness is not just in thought but is an activity that produces something fully alive in us. Self-forgiveness dealt with the tormenting thoughts in my head and heart. This was a real encounter with God by letting Him love me. Anytime I can't control my thoughts, I shift my focus to Him. I choose to receive His love. When I let God love me, it breaks the shame. (End of Harold Eberle quote.)

Every journey is unique because each individual is unique. I trust that Harold's story will be helpful to many. It illustrates powerfully that brain activities and the capability to change the way we think is within one's power. New thoughts, emotions and feelings will create a new future story. A powerful, life-focused, promise-filled future is the original design from the beginning. This is the Creator's design for each person. This is the Creator's design for you.

Each individual must find the specific way to identify and deal with their personal hijackers. Most of the time, the assistance of other people will be necessary when dealing with the big intruders: anxiety, addiction, trauma and suicidal thinking. The primary source of the loss of control is either spiritual, psychological, biological or the combination of these areas. It is a combination unique to the individual journey, and fully under the redemptive power of the One who heals us.

## Summary

Some of the thoughts and ideas in this chapter are:

- Every human being is designed to flourish.
- Hope may get hijacked, future promises stolen.
- Major Violators: Anxiety, Addiction, Trauma and Suicide.
- Hijackers create "better place" illusions.
- Dark spiritual powers are against hope.
- Biology, psychology and spiritually of hope give insight into dealing with hijackers.
- Harold's story illustrates a way out of pain.
- Unforgiveness of self leads to torture.
- Every journey is unique with redemptive aspects.

Scripture referred to:  Matthew 18; Acts 27:20

**LET'S CONNECT TO DISCUSS THIS CHAPTER:**

**Join My Interactive Discussions:** Please come visit with me at www.IncreaseHope.com in section "Book Resources" where I will be posting specifically for this chapter. I invite you to leave your comments or questions and I'll personally be responding. I will also have audios and videos and other resources pertinent to the topics in this chapter.

**Join Our Live Events:** Carol and I also offer special events www.HopeAcceleratorSeminars.com for more personal and in-depth face to face training and equipping. I look forward to continued connection with you.

Blessings! - Arnold J. Allen

**Personal Notes**

_____
_____
_____
_____
_____
_____
_____
_____
_____
_____
_____
_____
_____
_____
_____
_____
_____
_____
_____
_____
_____
_____
_____
_____
_____
_____
_____
_____

To change our lifestyle—our hope-style—it is necessary to change our core beliefs to become congruent with truth not myth.

*And patience produces character, and character produces hope. And this hope will never disappoint us....*

Romans 5:4-5 (NCV)

# 11
# Co-Creating Life

## The Domino Effect for Increasing Hope

Hope is injected into daily situations in a myriad of ways. Sometimes it is through small things, like the wedding invitation that I got in the mail today. A family friend in her forties will soon marry for the first time. Awesome! I am hopeful of the fulfillment that this relationship will bring into her life. At other times, hope seems more transcendent, such as praying with a friend who recently found that he has cancer.

Great or small, simple or profound, hope is a significant part of life. While co-creating life is essential for our species' survival, initiating hope is indispensable for our quality of life. Fostering and restoring hope demonstrates compassion—God's and ours.

## "Post-It" Hope

The late afternoon sun broke through the heavy cloud cover. Steam began to rise from the warming asphalt as the moisture evaporated following the heavy downpour. Two rainbows, increasing in brightness, hung in the clouds above the Alaskan airport as the pilot prepared for departure. Knowing that rainbows are signs of God's covenant promise, one wondered if something significant would happen on this trip. Would God visit the hospital tomorrow, showing up in remarkable ways? The rainbows vanished as the aircraft lifted into the dense cloud, carrying the Buckingham's on a mission trip.

The following day was a typical, bright southern California day, but the hospital room was heavy with sadness. Taking a breath and lifting her voice as though she was opening a window of the Spirit, Pastor Ellie began to speak words of life and encouragement. With deep resolve and firm power, the spoken Scriptures began to disperse the heaviness. Something intangible but significant was dissolving the sadness. God was working. Hope was demonstrating its power.

Our friends in Alaska, Pastors Don and Ellie Buckingham, had received a call from the daughter of a former church member. Her mom was in the hospital and failing rapidly. It seemed that she had lost the will to live. The Buckinghams felt to go to the California hospital and pray for this woman. On the way, God put a "Post It Note" plan in Ellie's heart. She began to write hope-filled scriptures on note cards. In the hospital room, she read these scriptures to the ill woman and then pinned the cards around the room. During subsequent visits, she read the cards to the woman. The nurses noticed the patient's response, picked up the idea and began to read the cards aloud as they cared for her. A will to live slowly rose in the ailing woman's heart. An amazing turnaround took place in a brief time. She became well and was soon released from the hospital. The power of authentic, transcendent hope had overcome her dire situation.

Hope comes from God. He instilled hope into our very essence when He breathed us into the womb. In response, we get to increase hope and foster it into a greater fullness, creating a hope response where none was evident. What Don and Ellie did for their friend was a type of creating. Similarly, we can "midwife" the creation of hope into another's life. As quoted above, "He has given us new birth into a living hope." As we communicate the gospel of Jesus Christ with others, we hold the door of hope open to them. God is the God of all hope. Jesus is the LIVING HOPE. The most hope-filled being in the universe is God Himself. When we create hope in others, we participate with God in restoring humanity.

## Resourcing the Power of the Word

The Scriptures were written to engender hope in our lives by revealing the character of God. When we see who He really is, we have hope for the future. Even in times of great distress, the Spirit of hope can bring us into a new place. In Lamentations 3, Jeremiah describes a season of great loss, pain and calamity. Then for a brief moment, the sun breaks through the darkened clouds and he sees a rainbow. The character of God is like a shaft of sunlight into the downpour of grief and loss.

The Message Bible puts it like this:

> But there's one other thing I remember, and remembering, I keep a grip on hope: God's loyal love couldn't have run out, his merciful love couldn't have dried up. They're created new every morning.

*How great your faithfulness! I'm sticking with God (I say it over and over). He's all I've got left. God proves to be good to the man who passionately waits, to the woman who diligently seeks. It's a good thing to quietly hope, quietly hope for help from God. It's a good thing when you're young to stick it out through the hard times.*

Lamentations 3:21-27

Jeremiah makes it clear that one of the ways to get through hard times is to remember who God is regardless of the circumstances. This is not a denial of the difficulty of the circumstances, nor is it merely positive thinking. Our friend Ellie changed the atmosphere of the hospital room as she read hope-filled scriptures. This happened, not just by reading the scripture, but because she had actually experienced the powerful truth of the verses being read. Her experience established a place of authority that is only obtained through living it. Our trials, tests, difficulties and pain are part of the process that establishes authority, character and hope in us. Ellie brought the God she knew into the room and into her friend's life. God did the rest as He had done with Jeremiah.

It is clear from Romans 5 that our response to suffering and trials is a source of hope creation. Conversely, if we hold the view that adversity is a negative thing, we will not find ourselves growing in hope. My son Aaron says, "Pain is my friend," when he is working out in the gym. This is the idea that Paul communicates in the scripture above. There is a purpose beyond what our current experience feels like. Fostering hope is like increasing muscle strength. The pain is a good sign. We can feel pain when we are trying to change, to be more hopeful. The more significant the change, the greater the pain. I am not suggesting that God causes pain in order for us to grow. I am saying that pain happens. When it does, allow the response to grow you and convey you into a greater knowledge of God.

As a farmer in my youth, I prepared the soil for a new crop by plowing the ground. The plowing is the first action—a hope action-—toward a new crop. The existing growth is turned under in expectation for the next season. Sometimes a healthy crop is plowed under as fodder for the next planting. Other times, the annual crop has been harvested and the land may be plowed or lay fallow for a year. The plow creates great turmoil as the atmosphere of the soil is changed. This turmoil of plowing is necessary for the next planting. Plowing is my friend. A new crop is in my future.

Authentic hope is often experienced like soil preparation. Whether the plow in soil, the pruning knife on the vine, or the axe from the American Idol judge, difficult changes create a new situation. Yet hope commands the new situation to flourish. The death of a vision is always the beginning of a new crop, a new season. Authentic, flourishing hope is the assurance of a fruitful future. As Romans 5 powerfully states, "This hope will never disappoint us" as the soil of the heart is prepared.

## The Experience/Truth Tension

We need to distinguish between experience and truth; the two are not synonymous. When we elevate experience equal to truth, we are in danger of destroying hope. Experience is real but not necessarily truth-based. Likewise, feelings are real but not necessarily in harmony with God's revealed truth. One goal of maturity is to increase the truth in our life experience. This will naturally reduce the life experiences that are not based on truth. John Sanford of Elijah House Ministries says that the role of the Christian counselor is to "evangelize the un-evangelized areas of the heart." Basically, he is saying that truth needs to enter and become active in aspects of our lives that have not yet received spiritual light. Truth tests experience.

The Message Bible says:

> *Grace and peace to you many times over as you deepen in your experience with God and Jesus, our Master. Everything that goes into a life pleasing God has been miraculously given us by getting to know, personally and intimately, the One who invited us to God.*

II Peter 1:2

Part of the maturing process is to bring our life experience into knowledge of God, both personally and intimately. Our lives are a process. Part of that process is to accept that we have not experienced the truth of God in every area of life. This is why we are seeking to experience Him, to know Him! The more that we come to know Him, the fewer problems we will have with deferred hope. A stronger hope creates a stronger love and faith experience. Understanding authentic hope is the key to mature growth in relationship.

As we understand the distinction between truth and experience, patterns of hope deferred will radically change. Because my dad was an alcoholic, I experienced emotional abandonment during a significant part of my formative years. The facts of my experience and feelings of abandonment are real to me. This actually happened and there are things that my family and I have to deal with because of it.

The tension that I deal with is therefore between the feelings of experience and the truth of my circumstances. I experienced abandonment; I felt deserted. These are real to me as a son of an alcoholic. The truth, however, is that my heavenly Father never abandoned me. The truth is that I was always in the presence of comfort and companionship. But in my ignorance, I did not know or fully access these things. I did not experience the level of comfort and companionship that I needed from God or others in the midst of the abandonment. Instead of accessing the energy of hope, I accessed the energy of anger. Even though I did not actually uncover these truths until years later, they were the truth for me at the time of pain. They are the truth for everyone alive. This is true for you. The more one comes to know these truths and bring experience and feelings into the truth, the more freedom and hope will be experienced.

Please hear me. I do not want to do some semantic shuffle. I do not want to create something that does not exist by using words differently. I want to create an effective way for anyone to walk out of the patterns and beliefs that impede hope. Both ultimate and finite hope can be engendered by truth. Experience and feelings can receive healing and comfort as God reveals Himself as our true caregiver.

Bondage occurs when we can not or will not access the truth

of authentic hope. As a young man, anger filled me to cover the pain of loss of my father's affection. Fortunately, Jesus told the story of the Good Samaritan to show how He cares for us and how we should care for each other. He described a trauma of physical injury and financial loss. PTSD, war, rape, or the loss to suicide may all fit this story. Experiences happen where we do not have the resources to recover. Although we have angels working with us, and the Spirit active in our circumstances, a key to fostering hope following trauma is to embrace God's truth for a specific need. Authentic hope is a bondage breaker.

## Partners in Hope-Creation

Observing the activity of God in people's lives creates hope within us. For decades, Mother Theresa of India was an inspiration for many. Her example of loving the poorest of the needy empowered others to reach out to those in need. Most of us do not encounter such severe need. Yet the principle of giving hope is the same for us as for Mother Theresa. When able, lend hope to others. When needed, receive hope yourself. Become a "hope generator," which in turn will attract help to the need. Partner with God.

We often forget this significant activity of hope. Hope attracts help. Remember this part of the hope definition (which I suggested earlier): "Hope carries an instinctive understanding of favorable treatment by God and others." Most of us have experienced situations where we threw our hands up crying: "This is hopeless! Forget trying to help!" Actually, our assessment of the situation may have been partially accurate.

When things are beyond help, the only possibility is hope. Our focus then needs to become the development of hope. When hope is manifest, it will attract help. The situation will change. Where there is need, help cannot be indifferent. Hope, by nature, has determined that things will change for the better. God is always hopeful and ready "to give you hope in your final outcome" (Jer. 29:11 AMP). He is our Help (Ps 42:5 NASB).

There is always hope. The hope that I am describing may not be in the present situation but it is always in us, and we need to find a way to infuse it into our circumstances. Ellie infused hope into the environment at the hospital. When we are without hope, we are forced to the One who always has enough hope. At times in my counseling office, situations are presented that are utterly hopeless. Certainly, every field of service has its practical limitations. So where do we go? What could possibly change our circumstances for the better? Since the absolute bottom line of hope is the person and character of God, there always is a place to go. I do not know what the answer will look like, but I do know Who it will reflect. Where there is God, there is hope. And God is everywhere.

The nature of hope is creative. It generates new ideas and creates energy to put those ideas into action. By this, hope creates an attraction to help. Appropriate ideas coupled with energy and resources equal help. Often, God brings help and deliverance through relationship. The Apostle Paul describes this interaction of help and hope when he tells of his mission trip to Asia. In II Corinthians 1:10-11 (NIV), he states: "On him we have set our hope that he will continue to deliver us, as you help us by your prayers." His hope is in God while an aspect of the help came from Paul's friends in Corinth. Sometimes practical help brings hope. At other times, it seems impossible to give help without first having a change in the hope level.

Dr. Groopman describes the influence of hope through a cancer survivor working with a struggling patient:

> Hope can be imagined as a domino effect, a chain reaction, each increment making the next increase more feasible. The familiar poetic phrase "hope flowers" captures this catalytic process. And the growth of hope is not strictly linear, always expanding. There are moments of fear and doubt that can deflate it, as when Dan left the hospital or entered the chemotherapy clinic. Deirdre Dolan, the oncology nurse, knew that more than words were needed. She purposefully positioned Dan next to Dotty Hirschberg and, by so doing, offered a model of hope to combat his despair. Dotty was living proof that a cure was possible. Her face finally replaced Tom Kane's in Dan's mind.

A few years earlier, Dan had accompanied his friend Tom as he lost a horribly painful fight with cancer. He pictured himself following the same course as Tom. Dotty created hope for Dan simply because she was a survivor. Through her hope, he began to believe that he could survive also.

The doctor instilled hope in a similar way for our daughter, Amiee, as she struggled with Chronic Fatigue Syndrome (CFS). He described his ability to overcome CFS in his own life. Now as an effective teacher and mother, Amiee is a model to others. As a survivor, she generates hope for those who battle CFS. Each time that we prevail over an enemy, we gain power and authority to influence others. Often, this influence gives others the courage and strength to endure. It is through our overcoming that help manifests.

## Fostering An Authentic Hope-Style

Remember the equation that I presented earlier in Chapter 3? Head knowledge plus heart values, fired in life experience, equals settled persuasion. Core values are the deep, core beliefs that get established in the heart and live out in relationship. Our lifestyle expresses those deep beliefs and values. To change our lifestyle—our hope-style—it is necessary to change our core beliefs. Our core beliefs must become congruent with truth not myth.

Obviously, not all beliefs are founded on truth. This is because not all experience is based on truth. Yet beliefs—whether based on truth or myth—energize our will. Therefore, in order to walk in truth and inspire hope in others, our beliefs must become truth-based, authentic and congruent with God.

Core beliefs are changed by receiving new truth intellectually, emotionally and spiritually. As new truth is revealed, our will is empowered for new choices. New experiences based on revealed truth establish new beliefs and values. This process is continually occurring in the context of evolving relationship. As we choose a positive response to truth, relationships mature in hope. This is the practical outworking of Romans 5:3-5 when proven character brings hope.

Because the process is relationship-based, the primary source of beliefs is our family of origin—the formative relationships closest to our hearts. Family generational lines carry a strong influence for or against hope. For example, comments like, "This is the most negative family that I have ever met," have lasting repercussions, not just on an individual level but also corporately, generationally. God wants to turn the course of a family toward hope-filled relationship. And as the family grows in expressing a powerful hope, God can multiply this grace into others.

To do this, tough choices must be embraced as we encounter myth in the family line. Authentic hope cannot be fostered when relationships are a vacuum consuming all our energy. Abuse, invalidation, manipulation and a variety of ill-treatment tactics is the bottomless pit that continually erodes the hope-building process. Healthy boundaries must be established and maintained. Relationships that do not conform to fostering hope must be distanced appropriately. Friends and family may not understand our journey as we embrace truth. However, they often appreciate the results. The fruit of tough choices is increased hope.

## Second Grade Hope

When our son Aaron was in a Canadian early elementary school, French was a required course. Due to a later diagnosed eye alignment issue, all school work was a big challenge. When his teacher suggested that he forgo the foreign language class to make the learning journey a bit easier, Aaron's response was quite the opposite. He questioned his mom, "How can I go on to college without taking a foreign language course?" Even though it was very difficult, Aaron pursued and successfully completed the required language requirement. As a child, he carried a hope within his heart to complete a college degree. Hope looks to the intended goal even if it is a decade in the future.

Aaron not only successfully completed the language requirements through high school, he went on to college and completed a B.A. in Business Administration. The hope of a second grader found fulfillment as an adult. Hope energized perseverance through the long journey. High hope is always equal to the goal.

## The Test of Finite Hope

We must establish boundaries to test our finite hopes.

> *Therefore gird up the loins of your mind, be sober, and rest your hope fully upon the grace that is to be brought to you at the revelation of Jesus Christ.*

> I Peter 1:13 (NKJV)

The Amplified Bible states it even more clearly:

> *So brace up your minds; be sober (circumspect, morally alert); set your hope wholly and unchangeably on the grace (divine favor) that is coming to you when Jesus Christ (the Messiah) is revealed.*

I recall being in a series of meetings where a very charismatic man was doing some heavy-handed fundraising. Not only was he "twisting the emotional arm" to convince people to give their money, he also had people "confessing" what they wanted to do for God financially. One elderly lady confessed to me that she expected to give a million dollars to the man's ministry. Knowing she was living on social assistance and without personal resources or gifting to handle significant funds. It felt like it was a false hope—even spiritual abuse, which is a prime breeding ground for deferred hope activity. Taking a good, critical look at core beliefs and values is essential for increasing the quality of hope. Beliefs and values are relationship boundaries.

## Surviving the Inertia

"Help!! I can't stop!! AAAAHHHHH!!" This was our inevitable cry just before the "head-over-heels" tumble through the pasture.

Walking home from an early summer fishing trip, my siblings and I crested the top of a steep hill in a neighbor's cattle pasture and challenged each other to a contest. The goal was to see who could run straight down the hill without falling. The prize was that the losers would carry the fishing gear home for the winner. As children, we did not understand Newton's laws of gravity acting on objects of mass. We simply knew that sometimes the hill was just too steep to navigate vertically. Somehow our bodies usually ended up moving faster than our legs could run, and the collapse into an uncontrolled somersault was unavoidable.

Although there was a powerful loss of control, the danger was minimal. It was usually limited to a few bumps and bruises. Occasionally, there was the need for a dip in the stream to wash off some cow dung. Of course, there was always the possibility of actually making the goal and lightening the load for the trip home. But the chance to experience inertia—one of the most powerful forces in physics—was what won over any fears we faced.

Today as an adult counselor, I often reflect on how the energy of the choices we make is like the "steep slope" contest of my childhood. It is as though our choices create energy of their own. It feels like we are overpowered by the force of our environment. The situation and the drive of those involved propel us beyond the limits of our resources. In times like these, we know instinctively that we are in for a fall, a smudge of cow dung, or worse. But we are caught up in the inertia—the natural resistance to change.

So how can we become free of the power that forces us into hurtful patterns?

It is often to identify the real source of the inertia that we are experiencing. As counselors, Carol and I are involved in helping people discover the sources that have contributed to problems, unfulfilled goals and relationship breakdowns. To gain understanding, we look at past experiences that produced conflict, misunderstanding and loss, probing with these inquiries.

- What were you hoping would come out of this?
- How did you anticipate that they [or God] would act?
- What things were done or not done that caused you pain or loss?

These and other questions are helpful in working through the source of energy contributing to destructive patterns. They facilitate renewal and deliverance from negative relationship.

Just as hope is a primary antidote to doubt, so it is undermined by core beliefs of doubt.

Core beliefs are formed in new environments, especially in our formative years. Our relational experiences tend to strongly influence the development of beliefs. From these, either hopeful or doubtful expectations may develop, depending upon our response and the reactions of our caregivers—the persons of authority in the situations. These expectations reactivate when we experience similar circumstances or feelings. As we act on the energy of these expectations, they form deep, valued beliefs.

In order to change, it is necessary to identify and change expectations. We do this by addressing the inertia—the energy forcing the patterns to repeat themselves. We must learn a way to run down the hill and stay upright. Fortunately, there is hope in spite of our limitations.

My friend May demonstrated a negative belief that, if she trusted God, she would be taken advantage of. Eventually, she realized that she always expected to be disappointed by God and men. It was a pattern of her life since childhood, and nothing on the horizon looked any different to her. The repeated experience of disappointment, coupled with the confusion of her ultimate and finite files, developed a reoccurring expectancy toward anything remotely male. (God is often viewed as male.)

So how can a mature believer who has walked with God for many years have this expectation? Quite easily. The expectation was mentored into her deep, core beliefs—her understanding of how life works. Mentoring (or training) is the process of teaching, demonstration and discipline; it is experience resulting in expectation. Experience is an effective teacher even when it teaches us the wrong things.

May's expectation had developed as a result of her life experiences. Her belief that God and men will let her down was trained into her from childhood. The expectation was the result of her experience and mentoring. Expectation has the power to mold, change and control. It has significant creative power. It increases or diminishes hope.

## The Ultimate Inertia: Experiencing God

God is intent upon conforming our expectations, and thus our beliefs, to His truth. Because expectations come from life experience, new experiences of God are necessary to form new expectations. As we discover God, we will change the expectations that are based on the experiences of not knowing Him. As part of that change, we receive revelation of His forgiveness, healing, love and comfort. These revelations carry an energy, an inertia, an impact, developing new and powerful core beliefs and values.

Through revelation, our expectations become attached to Him rather than to our former relationship experiences. We come to know Him as Father—God of all hope; Jesus—hope of our salvation; and Holy Spirit—the Spirit of hope. This knowledge is revealed in the head and the heart. Experiencing God enables our heart to abandon myth and create new beliefs. New beliefs result in new relationship. We begin to relate according to the revealed word of God. New relationships demonstrate life. Authentic hope flourishes in truth. Truth flourishes in authentic hope.

The most effective, lasting change comes by revelation. The Spirit reveals Biblical truth into our mind, heart and life experience. This is the most essential element in creating authentic hope. Over the past few years, I have found the Spirit leading me to pray for the Breath of God to breathe on a person's spirit. Requesting the Breath to come to the original place of hope often results in a renewing, hope-releasing experience. Sometimes it is sensed as a healing ointment. Other times, hope is manifest as comfort, rest and a settling peace. When the Breath of God brings hope, it always lifts heaviness, despair and anxiety. Even apathy and depression are altered in a significant, positive way. The most skewed myth is changed by the power of revealed, authentic hope.

> *A battered reed He will not break off, and a smoldering wick He will not put out, until He leads justice to victory. And in His name the Gentiles will hope.*
>
> Matthew 12:20-21 (NASB)

This is a type of revelation—a disclosing of who God is into the deep, foundational place of the heart. That which is barely alive is suddenly infused with hope energy. We begin to experience His presence in places that seemed abandoned, stuck, or left for dead.

Love's "hopes are fadeless under all circumstances" (I Corinthians 13:7 AMP). The God of love is also the God of all hope. As God increases the revelation of His love in our lives, hope also increases. The more that we know we are loved, the more we become people of hope. This is a synergetic relationship between hope, faith and love. The greatest of these is love. And love always hopes!

## Hope-Filled Thought and Emotion

Hope has a significant connection with the mind, for it is the place where hopeful thinking originates. Often, the critical contribution of the mind determines the quality of our hope. Stuck, locked-up, negative thoughts are hope killers. Creative, exploratory, positive thinking creates and strengthens hope. Imagination is an aspect of creative thinking. This ability to create ideas and images is a vital dimension of the hope process. In Lamentations 3, Jeremiah indicates that he has hope when he calls to mind the character of God. The focus of Jeremiah's thinking generates hope. Choosing to think and act differently contributes significantly to hope-filled experiences.

We experienced this with our daughter Amani who chose to go straight into college from grade ten, opening new and challenging possibilities for her life experience. Faced with the daunting prospects of such a test, she trained herself to think that she could survive college and actually flourish there. In response, something within her rose to the challenge. She eventually became an honor student and influenced the entire student body as editor of the college paper.

A mental picture of God joining our situation alters its anticipated outcome. Authentic hope paints a picture of a very different future for us. We begin to see ourselves in a different light. New, hope-filled pictures energize positive feelings.

One researcher describes this as "affective forecasting"—that is, the comforting, energizing, elevating feeling that we experience when we anticipate a positive future. Emotions and thoughts have a significant, intricate connection, which is manifest in hope.

Hope makes a person feel better. Hope creates a positive effect in our lives—spiritually, emotionally, mentally and physically. Through the Bible, God has done an outstanding job at describing the work of the Spirit in establishing hope in our lives. We can discover the power of hope by rereading the Bible as seen through the paradigm of the hope message. (Of course, reading my book will help as well. Just sayin.")

Just as hope makes us feel better, feeling better creates hope. Physical illness, changes in life, or simply not being in good, physical shape can significantly influence our sense of hope. This is true not only of the physical but also of our emotional and mental states. Tied closely with our internal sense of well-being, our financial situation and quality of relationships with others also creates or degrades hope. In order to increase hope, it is essential to change the areas of our life which are not hope-filled. The things that we cannot change require the power of hope to sustain us. Chronic illness, estranged relationships and other persistent situations may not be changeable. In order to feel better in these situations, a strategy of hope renewal is required.

As discussed earlier, hope has to do with our entire being—who we are in our true nature. Creating hope is not limited to a belief system and value development. As important as core beliefs are in our lifestyle, there are other dimensions to the hope equation. Remember Kathy? She was the hospital patient in a coma. The presence of her dog in the Intensive Care room initiated a significant change, pulling her from the edge of death to the shores of life. Sometimes creating hope even requires us to get out and connect with nature, standing under a waterfall or observing a rainbow. Make it a point to regularly refresh your hope creating sources.

## Summary

Some of the things that we have looked at related to creating hope:

- God is the primary creator of hope.
- Scriptures create and increase hope.
- We have the capacity to create hope in others.
- Hope attracts help.
- A right response to suffering and trial create hope.
- Finite hope requires boundaries or tests.
- Experience must be weighted against or filtered by truth.
- Changing core beliefs and values is vital in creating hope.
- Inertia of expectations is powerful and make or break hope.
- Ultimate inertia: Experiencing God is a key to revelation.
- Revelation by the Holy Spirit is an essential in the pursuit of Biblical hope.
- Hope heals and supports the sense of well-being.
- Feeling better & thinking better create hope.

Scriptures important to creating hope:

Psalms 42:5, 46:1; Jeremiah 29:11; Lamentations

3:21-27; Matthew 12:20-21; Romans 5:3-5, 15:4; 1 Corinthians 13:7; II Corinthians 1:10-11; Titus 3:7; 1 Peter 1:3, 13; II Peter 1:2

## LET'S CONNECT TO DISCUSS THIS CHAPTER:

**Join My Interactive Discussions:** Please come visit with me at www.IncreaseHope.com in section "Book Resources" where I will be posting specifically for this chapter. I invite you to leave your comments or questions and I'll personally be responding. I will also have audios and videos and other resources pertinent to the topics in this chapter.

**Join Our Live Events:** Carol and I also offer special events www.HopeAcceleratorSeminars.com for more personal and in-depth face to face training and equipping. I look forward to continued connection with you.

Blessings! - Arnold J. Allen

## *Personal Notes*

God intends to "co-create" a future story with us.

*May the God of hope fill you with all joy and peace as you trust in him, so that you may overflow with hope by the power of the Holy Spirit.*

Romans 15:13 (NIV)

# 12
# Nurturing Hope

## The Care and Feeding of the Hope Atmosphere

As we restore hope, we embark on a perpetual journey of developing our future story. The essential focus of hope restoration is discovering how our future is influenced by our past. What of our past experiences is defining how we will experience the future? Where are the hope places that are now sources of pain, anxiety and apprehension? How do I hope again when the most precious thing in my life has died? And what do I do about the patterns of response that have eroded my self-image under a deluge of abusive words and actions?

**Webster's Dictionary:**

sto•ry  n

> 1. a factual or fictional account of an event or series of events

"Well, I may as well start at the beginning...." With this opening, the account of events unfolds. We all have our "series of events," our side of things, our story. The elements of the accounts are the way we remember them. Sometimes elements get lost or distorted over time. We live with it the way that we remember it. This is important because our memory of the past significantly influences our future story. We tend to project what the future will be, based on our past experience. Specifically, the memories of our experiences become the foundation of our choices. We develop a story in our minds of what will be lived out in our future. And then we live it.

As we have learned in the first parts of this book, God wants to show up in our lives. He wants us to confidently expect His goodness (hope) so He can do new things in our lives (faith). He really, really cares about every person (love). Obviously, the future will have elements of the past. Some of our past experiences inspire the hope story. There will be new things in our future, new experiences, new revelation. Yet the amount of newness will depend a lot on us. God has already determined to contribute.

> *"For I know the plans I have for you," declares the Lord, "plans to prosper you and not to harm you, plans to give you a hope and a future."*
>
> Jeremiah 29:11 (NIV).

I think He intends to contribute a lot. What do you think?

Seriously, we each need to examine this question. What do we think God wants to contribute to our life experience that will make our future different than our past? Obviously, God intends to "co-create" a future story with us. Fortunately, the principle contribution is Himself. He is a God of relationship and is very interested in growing the relationship with us. New things will come with the relationship, but as I pointed out in the Christmas story with Carol and Autumn, these things will be about relationship. God has the same priorities for you and I as we saw in Carol's gift to her granddaughter. It was similar for Molly, Tim, Sarah and Amari, Henry and many other stories that I have reported here. He wants to deepen our relationship with Him and often He uses the things that we desire to strengthen that relationship.

One common hindrance to authentic hope, especially in relationship to God, is the contamination of our ultimate hope understanding. The fruit of this contamination: fear, confusion and disillusionment, may make hope unattainable. Finding and dealing with the source of the contamination requires the Spirit, the scriptures, mentors and healers who will work with us in renewing our spirit, mind and heart. Although I have been viewing our personal design as holistic, it may be helpful to address three aspects considered in Chapter 6: The Psychology of Hope, The Biology of Hope and The Spirituality of Hope. We can identify aspects in each dimension for cleansing and renewal in the hope-building journey.

## The Spirituality of Hope

In considering the role of the spirit in the hope journey, I want to look at three key components of the personal spirit. I will describe the activities of the various dimensions of the spirit as well as the care and feeding of each. For the purpose of facilitating hope in relationships, I consider intuition, premonition and conscience to be activities of the personal spirit.

## 1. Intuition: Gut Hope

Intuition is a function of the personal spirit. The normal activity of intuition is instinctive understanding, sensitivity, inklings, discernment, perception and insight. These are aspects of intuition that every individual possess to some degree. Some are born with a natural tendency to engage this aspect of their spirit. Others develop an intentional awareness of this activity. Regardless, everyone, male or female, is intuitive to some extent. In various ways, this activity of the spirit either gets developed or repressed. When it is repressed, the intuitive dimension may become skewed, clouded or silent from the toxicity that diminishes its influence. Often, the power of the reasoning mind dulls or freezes the intuitive activity. Insensitivity, indifference, and dullness of spirit make the natural intuition voiceless to inform the mind and body of spiritual insight.

An active intuition is key to an awareness of our own state of hopefulness. This spiritual activity is able to discern our increasing or decreasing hope attitude and presence. It enables self-awareness so that hope remains healthy and fed. This is as natural to the spirit as hunger is to the stomach. When we feel hungry, we eat. When the spirit is sensing hopelessness or anxiety, it needs fed as well.

Intuition is also vital to perceiving hope in another person. Through an instinctive understanding or awareness, the quality of hope in another person may be discerned. Insight into the need of people provides the opportunity to help them. The intuitive spirit thrives on nurturing, both to give and receive authentic hope.

Invalidation is harmful to intuition. Certain statements and questions can undermine the energy of the spirit.

"Why do you feel that way?"

"Where do you come up with these ideas?"

"You shouldn't be so sensitive!"

A refreshing, cleansing action must be initiated at a fundamental level of spirit activity to eliminate the effects of these corrosive inquiries. Validation, affirmation and blessing are important aspects of restoring the spirit.

## 2. Premonition: Reading the Future

Premonition is another function of the personal spirit. The activity of premonition is a forewarning, foreboding, foretelling, a sense of something to come. Although neither positive nor negative by nature, premonition is still often associated with something unpleasant about to happen. To some degree, the personal spirit visits future events. The future-oriented insight of premonition gives the opportunity to release hope into the unfolding future. It also provides the opportunity to prepare a robust hope prior to difficult events.

Carol and I once had counseling offices about 20 minutes from our home. We often worked together counseling certain clients. During the short trip from our home, we began to experience various emotions or attitudes between us. Tension, anger, anxiety and a variety of other emotions cropped up in our casual conversation. These were not part of our normal communication. Upon arrival, we would clear up our relationship the best that we could before meeting with clients, but we were still mystified about a reason for the sudden negativity. Then we began to identify a pattern. The conflicting issues that we experienced on our way to the session were the same issues that needed to be dealt with at the session. We realized that our hearts were extended toward the next clients and we were experiencing the premonition of coming issues that would arise in the counseling session. This discovery empowered us with increased hope as we worked with pre-session briefings from our spirit. And it made our commute much more enjoyable.

A similar type of reading the future can occur as we prepare for an event, gathering or fellowship time. The anticipation in our spirit gives us a sense of how the experience will be. This aspect of hope can be strengthened and developed as we tune in to our inner voice. As we strengthen and validate this connection, we are enabled and prepared by premonition for the intentional release of hope.

The activity of premonition within our spirit is often joined by God's Spirit. At times, it is not clear whether the future insight that I am describing is of ourselves or the Spirit. As we embrace spirit to Spirit communion, there is a steady flow of insight from the Spirit of hope, the Spirit of future promise. This flow empowers confidence as we move into the unfolding future. The quality of premonition is enhanced by God's Spirit.

## 3. Conscience: Clean Energy

Conscience is another dimension of the personal spirit. The

activity of the conscience is to inform the mind of what is right and wrong, thereby governing thoughts and actions. The original state of a healthy spirit impels one to do right rather than wrong. This is especially true of the heart filled with God's love. This is a very hope-filled, hope-energized view of life. Hope pursues a passion for purity. Purity inspires the energy of hope.

> *And everyone who has this hope fixed on Him purifies himself, just as He is pure.*
>
> 1 John 3:3 (NASB).

The context of this scripture is set in the discussion of relationship. It concerns having a passion to be like the One we love. Authentic hope has a pure conscience and energizes the will toward loving choices. Hope enhances our relationship with Jesus as well as others. A conscience free from condemnation fosters the spirit-to-Spirit relationship, as well as the spirit-to-spirit relationship.

Consciences come in a variety of conditions, depending on our overall spiritual state. The scriptures describe various states of the conscience as weak, defiled, evil and seared with a hot iron, as well as good, pure and cleansed. One's conscience is cleansed, purified and brought into alignment through revealed truth in intimate relationship with *the* Truth, *the* Living Hope.

> *How much more shall the blood of Christ, who through the eternal Spirit offered Himself without blemish to God, cleanse your conscience from*

*dead works to serve the living God.*

Hebrews 9:14 (NASB)

Cleansing the conscience empowers the spirit to move from doing dead works to releasing life energizing, authentic hope.

## Influencing Spirits

A common hindrance to hope is the work of spiritual powers against us. Because spiritual warfare happens in the realm of finite activities, the enemy opposes us as we endeavor to live for God, or even ourselves. Sometimes this is a pervasive kind of thing as I described with Judy after the loss of her nine-year-old daughter. In that case, it was as though dark angels rode on the energy of the deep, normal grief associated with this staggering loss. At other times, the resistance may be more subtle. A blocking spirit or dark sentinel may be sent to keep us from seeing a certain aspect of God's character, creating a foothold for hope to be deferred and ultimate hope contaminated.

In contrast, the Spirit of truth leads us into all truth. This leading is into revelation. It is into a knowing that alters our experience of bondage and defeat, thus empowering a future filled with promise. Rather than dark spirits, angelic messengers may be used by the Spirit to provide help like they did for Jesus before his crucifixion. When we experience the help of God, hope is increased. Embracing revealed truth will always increase authentic hope.

## The Psychology of Hope

As suggested in Chapter 6, The Psychology Of Hope is

focused primarily on the mind and emotions. The study of hope is a recent activity in psychology but has become a significant topic of interest. Research shows that high-hope people do better in school, are ill less often, recover from illness more quickly, take on more complex tasks and have longer lasting relationship. (They also write better books.) While the primary focus of psychology addresses finite hope, the principles of renewal and strengthening the hope journey are the same for ultimate hope.

Some key aspects of feeding a hopeful atmosphere include goal assessment and adjustment. High-hope people pursue goals created in their own heart and mind. My friend and Bible teacher Ted Hanson says, "We always do what we want to. So God, help me change my 'want to'!"  The most effective goals are internal, self-set goals. These are specific, short term goals rather than vague, long term goals. Mastery goals (the knowledge and skill that allows you to do, use or understand something very well) or learning goals are more effective than performance and achievement goals. Well-completed goals add value to life as well as get things accomplished.

Another key is that high-hope individuals tap into their motivational resources and support. They employ the skill of accessing both the inner energy of hope as well as gaining strength and energy from others. There is a community element in an authentic hope journey. High-hope individuals are part of a creative flow of energy in a network of relationships, giving to and gaining from relationship. The care and feeding of authentic hope includes identifying and accessing supportive energies of a supportive community.

A third key in The Psychology Of Hope is to assess the quality of one's thoughts. High-hope people develop and foster positive thoughts about the unfolding future. Whether recovering from injuries, writing a dissertation, or dealing with job stress, hope-filled thinking releases positive energy into future events and relationships with beneficial results. Identifying and changing negative, low-hope thinking and self-talk patterns are essential elements in developing a more hope-filled lifestyle—our hope-style.

A specific part of the hopeful thinking process concerns options and alternatives. High-hope people assume that a variety of pathways are available to reach a goal. When obstacles hinder progress, creative alternatives are developed. When overcoming an obstacle or selecting a new path, high-hope people find ways to reach the goal. Learning to discover multiple pathways increases hope possibilities. Creative options and alternative ways to move ahead spring from authentic hope.

## The Biology of Hope

In Chapter 5, I presented some research that described the powerful influence referred to as the placebo and nocebo response. I also suggested that cells, especially those massed in a specific organ, contain a type of memory influencing the whole person. This information is helpful in understanding the biological resource in the care and feeding of authentic hope.

The power of the placebo response may be harnessed in the care and feeding of authentic hope. When coupled with a protocol—a specific procedure—expectation and belief [hope] gain power. Administered by an authority, this combination produces an outcome in the body so powerful that it can duplicate a drug result. The application for our discussion is the amazing power of our being when spirit, soul and body come into an agreed harmony toward a focused outcome. Creating a protocol fortifies the outcome of our actions. This alignment of spirit, soul and body is in cooperation with an authority— God's word and Spirit. When our routine is expectation and anticipation of a good outcome, authentic hope is fostered.

The fact that researchers endeavored to duplicate the effects of a drug is a side issue. The central insight drawn from these studies is that there exists a harmony of being that is powerful in its ability to achieve a goal. The energy of the personal spirit, the force of neurotransmitters in the brain, the power of emotion and the strength of the body united move us toward a focused outcome. This activity of hope is breathed on by the Spirit, thus producing a result greater than the human effort. Greater harmony in our being produces greater power of hope.

Body memory, a key resource for hope, should not be overlooked. The memories and experiences that are stored in the body become a resource to draw upon and to manifest. Earlier, I illustrated the ability of the physical heart to hold memory. The memories of physical sensations in intimate worship—times of God's physical comfort or peace—are all sources of hope. The hug of a friend, a dad's kiss on the forehead or a supportive look from a loved one releases support into our being. Recalling these physical memories energizes the hope experience.

Brain research shows that people who engage in prayer or meditation daily strengthen their anterior cingulate cortex (ACC) a part of the prefrontal cortex where the brain registers the experience of love, compassion and empathy. The healthier your ACC is, the more calm your brain's amygdala (the alarm center in your limbic system) will be, thus decreasing the amount of fear and anxiety you'll experience. Less fear, more hope! This process is also activated when we receive prayer from a trusted individual. More prayer and meditation, more hope!

Corrie ten Boom was a prisoner in a Nazi concentration camp. To create a place of rest and comfort, she would recall and experience a certain childhood memory. As a child, her father would pray for her each night when he put her to bed. His custom was to place his large hand gently over her whole face. As an adult, her whole person was flooded with peace and rest as she recalled her father's touch. She began to experience the hand of her heavenly Father much the way her dad had touched her. The recall of this physical-based memory sustained hope when she did not know if the next day would bring the gas chamber. The physical sensations in her face became a source of hope.

A nocebo response is the body's ability to duplicate the expected negative side effects of a drug. Nocebo demonstrates scientifically that the focus on a negative image or trait is duplicated in one's life experience. We manifest what we focus upon. The focused energy on a negative trait, even if we are trying to rid ourselves from it, can actually strengthen its hold. We may end up putting more energy into trying to overcome the negative than into building the desired character.

Energy produces fruit. The greatest fruitfulness comes from a focus on positive characteristics rather than the negative.

## Hope Builders

Testimony of the works of God also nourishes hope. As accounts of salvation, healing, deliverance, provision and other releases by God's hand are declared, expectation is increased in the listener's heart. We often hear this called "building your faith," but from a Biblical understanding, this is building hope. It is the increase of a confident expectation that God will show up and do good things among us. As hope increases, an atmosphere for faith is created. When God does speak or act, the hope-filled heart is in a posture to receive. A new testimony is created.

The role of personal prophecy is often used in a similar, hope building way. Prophecy in word, song, dance or art will result in the expectation of God's presence increasing or becoming manifest in tangible ways. This expectation is an invitation to the Spirit. It is like a gentle rain softening the soil of the heart and mind. The spirit of prophecy encourages and builds people up. "One who prophesies speaks to people for their strengthening, encouraging and comfort" (1 Corinthians 14:3 NIV). In this atmosphere of expectant energy, the manifest presence of God often increases. This Spirit of prophecy—the Spirit of Jesus—is the Spirit of hope.

There is a synergy that happens in the flow of the Spirit. As people praise, worship, prophesy and participate in other expressions of God's presence, His presence becomes more manifest, experienced by more people. This is an aspect of His glory and anointing. This type of manifest glory builds hope while purging shame and hopelessness. There is a significant increase in the expectation of God's activity in the midst of this spiritual atmosphere.

God's presence may become tangible in the form of hard, physical evidence. Healing, deliverance and salvation take place as a result of being in the presence of God. Aside from freeing the oppressed individual, these physical manifestations build hope. They increase expectation. They increase anticipation. They provide a physical dimension of glory to the environment. They also demonstrate that the veil between earth and heaven is thin. God's presence increases authentic hope.

When our daughter Amani was a teenager, she was diagnosed with scoliosis, a curvature of the spine. She came to us one day saying that Benny Hinn, a Christian evangelist and spiritual healer, would be holding meetings in Portland, Oregon. She felt that God was saying that if we attended the meetings, she would be healed. We were about a six hour drive from Portland and agreed to go. As we entered the packed stadium, I could feel the atmosphere electric with anticipation. The hope was almost tangible; it was so energized. Carol and I, as thousands of others, were filled with hope. We knew that God loved being with His people and wonderful things happen in His presence. Amani was filled with faith. She knew what God was about to do and when it would take place.

As we gathered for the second or third meeting, Amani said that the ministry would happen at 10:00 that evening and that she would be the first or second one called out for ministry. Sure enough, when Benny started the healing time, it was 10:00 and the first or second word he gave was for healing scoliosis. The power of God came upon Amani and she was touched with a healing presence. Although it took an outworking of the process, she was completely healed and remains healed nearly twenty years later. The atmosphere of authentic hope in the gathering provided an environment for faith to manifest. By putting oneself in a hope-generating environment, increased hope is refreshed and fostered.

## The Hope of Heaven

One very significant element of fostering a hope filled atmosphere is its connection to heaven. There is a reality to the hope of eternal life. As Romans 8 clearly states, "we hope for what we do not see, for what we do not yet have." We are drawn toward the future, including the eternal, by this expectation. Every person has a seed, a deposit of the future, as part of his or her makeup. Through a personal relationship with Jesus, that seed births access to eternal life. It starts here, flourishes here and finds its fulfillment in heaven.

Successful restoration and nurturing of a hope-filled mind and heart will be specific to each of us. Many elements of life influence our hope experience. The structure of right-brain or left-brain people impacts how we acquire hope. Our relationship to nature influences hope development. The expression of various art forms contribute to the hope-filled lifestyle. By nature, hope is creative. Obstruction in creativity often results in a hindrance to the restoration and nurturing of hope. Fortunately hope looks past hindrances and pursues restoration and nurturing through many ways within each individual.

Everyone has the innate capacity to be hope-filled and hope

givers. The areas of greatest hindrance can become a source of insight and strength for your own life as well as the lives of those that you influence.

Some aspects of restoring and nurturing hope are:

- With God we co-create our future story.
- Spirituality of hope is personal spirit and God's Spirit.
- Intuition can sense hope in oneself and others.
- Premonition releases hope into the unfolding future.
- Clear conscience fosters the spirit of authentic hope.
- Dark spiritual powers work against hope.
- Psychology of hope is the mind and emotions.
- Biology of hope is energy in the physical body.
- Testimony and prophecy bring nourishment to hope.
- God's manifest glory nurtures hope.
- Heaven is a hope-filled connection.

Scriptures referred to in this chapter are from the NIV:

> Job 11:18, 14:7; Psalms 31:24, 62:5; Proverbs 23:18; Isaiah 42:3; Jeremiah 29:11; Romans 8, 15:13; 1 Corinthians 14:3; Titus 1:2; Hebrews 9:14, 11:1; 1 Peter 1:3, 1 John 3:3.

## LET'S CONNECT TO DISCUSS THIS CHAPTER:

**Join My Interactive Discussions:** Please come visit with me at www.IncreaseHope.com in section "Book Resources" where I will be posting specifically for this chapter. I invite you to leave your comments or questions and I'll personally be responding. I will also have audios and videos and other resources pertinent to the topics in this chapter.

**Join Our Live Events:** Carol and I also offer special events www.HopeAcceleratorSeminars.com for more personal and in-depth face to face training and equipping. I look forward to continued connection with you.

Blessings! - Arnold J. Allen

***Personal Notes***

_____

_____

_____

_____

_____

_____

_____

_____

_____

_____

_____

_____

_____

_____

_____

_____

_____

_____

_____

_____

_____

Authentic hope is the brave power to show up with expectation and be present in any given life situation.

*But we have this treasure in earthen vessels, so that the surpassing greatness of the power will be of God and not from ourselves.*

II Corinthians 4:7 NASB

# 13
# Reflections On the Future

## Ruminations Of Things To Come

A couple of years ago, in the beautiful rolling hills of northern Idaho, our youngest son Aaron married Anna. The rural retreat center where the wedding was held was filled with family and friends gathered from far and wide. Although the region had suffered a serious windstorm just a week earlier, the power was back on, water was running and rooms were prepared. A temporary patch covered a gaping hole in the roof where a large tree had taken its toll. A full day of arranging chairs, setting up tables, stringing lights and festive decorations transformed the common meadow into a celebrated, sacred space. Huge fluffy clouds floated through the blue sky as the wedding ceremony and dinner were enjoyed.

As we prepared to transition from dinner to dance, dark clouds began to roll over the hill as the wind rapidly shifted from a gentle breeze to a hurricane force. We raced to rescue tables, chairs and décor. The wind and rain forced us from the patio into the lodge. With the appearance that the reception was ruined, the bride's heart sank and her tears flowed. What now? As a tree toppled in the yard, the owner informed us that we needed to vacate the building. The trees surrounding the lodge were so large that one could crush the place if it came down. As we were herded from the lodge into the garden area sheltered from the powerful wind, the heavy rain had turned to a light drizzle. Within a few minutes, one of Aaron's groomsmen, Jonathan, drove his car to the garden. Swinging the hatch open and turning the CD player to max volume, he announced the first dance. Aaron and Anna had their first dance in the rainy garden.

With some improvising of the RV generator, the dance floor was lit, the sound system energized and the party went on for hours. In the tension of the moment, Jonathan's quick decision ignited hope—dance-in-the-rain hope! The first dance led to the whole gathering celebrating. The storm's destruction gave way to the celebration of relationships. We celebrated Aaron, Anna and each other. We celebrated life.

As I conclude this book, I would underline the reality that hope is founded in relationship. All of the life stories I have included— all of the good and bad situations and all of the painful losses— are to illustrate the power of authentic hope. We do not always have a groomsman like Jonathan to rally the cause. We may not have a dance partner to twirl us across the floor. The storm may have taken our resources, our home, our spouse, our child or our health. Yet we always have hope. The experience of getting "thrown under the bus" is an overwhelming, painful reality. In the pain, we may become blinded to the greater reality of transcendent hope. Yet, there is hope—*authentic, dance-in-the-rain hope for the unfolding future.*

Hope is as certain as the blood flowing through your veins. Put your fingers on your pulse. If you can feel it, there is hope somewhere in your being. Where there is life, there is hope. Even when all appears dead as a tree stump, there is hope. In a simple childlike way, Molly Hogan was able to experience hope as a person—Jesus. Her openness of spirit engaged hope both in her and in her dad. It is not easy for an adult to access that level of openness of spirit, but it is possible. I can do it and you can do it. *Hope is present even in the insurmountable pain of the unfolding future.*

Hope is flowing toward each of us every moment of every day. If we are in a good life experience, hope flows through us to others. If things are going well and falling into place, we have hope to give away. Go change a life. Sometimes hope is given in a gift, a smile, a hug or a simple look in the eye. Experience the reality that hope attracts help. When you give hope to others, help will follow. When we allow hope to flow from others into our lives, favor follows. Give hope away! Receive hope! Keep the flow going! *The flow empowers the unfolding future!*

You are favored! You are a uniquely designed, one of a kind, irreplaceable! You cannot figure this out—it has to be accepted. If your heart is beating, you have favor! If you have flesh and bones, you are favored! You will never come to this conclusion by comparing yourself with another or even who you think you should be. Every day, someone is thinking good thoughts towards you. Every day that you draw breath is a day of favor and hope. The Bible says that it is better to be a live dog than a dead lion; better to have a little bit of hope than none at all. If you know the favor I am describing, give it to others. Giving favor fosters hope, and hope attracts help. Hope is contagious. *Favor and help facilitate the unfolding future.*

In reality, a lion is much more powerful than a dog. You may be a lion in your home, community or other spheres of influence. Authentic hope empowers everyday folks to be agents of positive change in their arena of influence. You are the conduit. You carry the frequency of hope into the environment. Your life influences the atmosphere wherever you are. The limitless nature of hope is always looking for an increased expression and manifestation. New ideas are always linked to the hope-supply, and the hope-supply is limitless. Increased activation is an invitation to the hope-flow. Thinking outside the box summons hope. To conceive of things being different; to imagine alternative conclusions; to formulate a picture of what could be beyond the horizon—facilitate hope. *This is hope possessing the unfolding future.*

Hope creates space for a new conversation. Hope expects new thoughts, new words and new ideas. Hope is a bit like an iceberg. We experience a measure but the bulk of hope is in the unseen, the unexperienced, the yet-to-be-discovered. Hope fosters vulnerability, risk and pursuit of the unknown. All healthy relationships maintain these characteristics. Hope embodies living wholeheartedly. Hope is not the assurance of victory but the courage to step into the battle. This is the hope that cloaked Sarah as she faced the uncertainty of surgery on little Amari. A settled peace filled Sarah in the midst of an unsettled situation. Only God knows the depth of the unseen spirit and the full purpose of each life. With "eternity" scripted in their DNA, *Amari Faith and her family were possessing the unfolding future.*

Tenacious hope is in everyone's DNA. This vulnerable, gritty, passionate energy knows that you are stronger than you think you are. It is the energy that American Idol contestant Danny Gokey sung about, that which has carried him into the unfolding future. It is the tenacity that carried my mom through decades of life as the spouse of an abusive alcoholic. It is the energy that rose up from the depth of Deborah Crone as she and David walked away from the hospital room leaving the dead body of their daughter behind. "I will not live mad and I will not live sad," Deborah declared to the unfolding future. This tenacious hope is energizing Henry as he invests his life into the unfolding future of Budapest, Katmandu and Kampala pastors. Authentic hope is the brave power to show up with expectation and be present in any given life situation. To risk it all in hope is to let go of the present reality in order to lay hold of a greater potential reality. Hope is always brave. *Bravery is a requirement in possessing the unfolding future.*

Dance in the rain!

Live vulnerable! Live limitless!

Live tenacious! Live brave! Live strong!

*Possess the unfolding future!*

## LET'S CONNECT TO DISCUSS THIS CHAPTER:

**Join My Interactive Discussions:** Please come visit with me at www.IncreaseHope.com in section "Book Resources" where I will be posting specifically for this chapter. I invite you to leave your comments or questions and I'll personally be responding. I will also have audios and videos and other resources pertinent to the topics in this chapter.

**Join Our Live Events:** Carol and I also offer special events www.HopeAcceleratorSeminars.com for more personal and in-depth face to face training and equipping. I look forward to continued connection with you.

Blessings! - Arnold J. Allen

***Personal Notes***

_____

_____

_____

_____

_____

_____

_____

_____

_____

_____

_____

_____

# ABOUT THE AUTHOR

## Arnold J. Allen

Born and raised in the mountains of northern Vermont, Arnold had

planned to work the family dairy farm but opted for Nazarene Bible College in Colorado Springs. Graduating the youngest

in his class, at 20 years of age Arnold, his wife Carol and young son, A.J. took on the responsibility of pastoring a church in New Brunswick, Canada. While hosting Youth With A Mission (YWAM) teams, in 1976 they decided to focus on discipleship and evangelism with the Mission. After nearly two decades in missions and international travel, Arnold returned to school to complete a Master of Counseling program at Trinity Western University in Langley, B.C. Canada in 1998.

The Allen's have received training in Canada and South Africa with the Neethling Brain Instruments. This cutting edge thinking preference profile has proven effective in education, vocational selection, sports effectiveness training, business and hundreds of other applications.

Among various applications, Arnold and Carol have found it to be a fruitful marriage and relationship communication tool.

Caring for people through counseling, training and hope building activities, they contribute love, wisdom and focused understanding to individuals, families and the community. They are often looked to as a father and mother in their circles of relationships.

Arnold J. Allen is an author, speaker and educator. He and his wife Carol are the directors of Increase Hope Foundation, a non-profit, charitable 501(c) 3 organization in development and reside in Washington State. They enjoy life with their local community, four children and 12 grandchildren. They are available for local and international bookings.

For more information, please visit www.IncreaseHope.com for bookings and interviews.

# Appendix A

## Hebrew Terms for Hope

A variety of Hebrew terms are used to convey hope. I will discuss some of the key ones. You may find words with similar meaning in your concordance under words such as: confidence, trust and wait. Developing a working, Biblical definition of hope involves some degree of understanding of terms but the essential requirement is revelation by the Spirit.

Key characteristics of Hebrew terms include:

- *Tiqvah* (tik•vä' 34 times) Positive, intuitive, existing yet abstract; Resists limits, common to all living things, universal; Doesn't need to be acquired, just is, innate. (Strong's H8615)
- *'achariyth* (akh•ar•ēth' 66 times) A future reward, latter end. This word is translated sometimes as hope or future hope. (Strong's H319)

*Tiqvah* speaks of hope as something meaningful and solid. Absolutely everybody and every living thing possesses hope. The poor have hope (Job 5:16), the afflicted have it (Ps 9:18) and even a tree has it (Job 14:7). There is a different fate for the hope of the wicked from the righteous. "When a wicked man dies, his expectation [*tiqvah*] will perish; and the hope of strong men perishes." (Proverbs 11:7 NASB)

In the poetry of the Psalms, we discover that hope comes from God Himself. "Yes, my soul, find rest, in God; my hope [*tiqvah*] comes from him" (Psalms 62:5 NIV). In the even more specific perspective of Psalms 71:5 (NIV), "For you have been my hope [*tiqvah*], Sovereign Lord, my confidence since my youth." We can be confident that this hope will never be taken from us. Proverbs 23:17-18 (NIV): "Do not let your heart envy sinners, but always be zealous for the fear of the Lord. There is surely a future hope [*'achariyth*] for you, and your hope [*tiqvah*] will not be cut off."

In a number of scriptures the Hebrew word "achariyth is translated as "future hope." The Amplified Bible translates it as "latter end" (a future and a reward). This is a good rendition of what *'achariyth* actually means. The ultimate outcome of a situation, even the possible eventuality of still undetermined circumstances, is within the scope of hope.

> *"For I know the plans that I have for you," declares the Lord, "plans to prosper you and not to harm you, plans to give you hope [tiqvah] and a future ['achariyth]."*
>
> Jeremiah 29:11 (NIV)

> *"There is hope [tiqvah] for your future ['achariyth]," declares the Lord. "And your children will return to*

*their own territory."*

Jeremiah 31:17 (NASB)

To sum up, *tiqvah* is positive, intuitive and definite. For Job it is not absurd to ascribe the possession of tiqvah to a tree. In the Psalms God alone is the source of *tiqvah* and God is Himself *tiqvah*. For Jeremiah *tiqvah* and *'achariyth* are inseparable in God's blessings upon His people. This hope [*tiqvah*] requires neither faith nor even effort to acquire—it simply is.

Hope is also used in a verb form. A frequently used verbal form of hope is yachal.

> *Yachal* (yä•khal' 45 times) To expect; Utter dependence, without understanding of what's happening, implicit trust; To wait. (Strong's H3176)

Some of the uses of the term are translated "hope in." In the midst of Job's suffering there was an inability in his friends to provide him with comfort or an adequate explanation of his loss. Job exclaims, "Though he slay me, yet will I hope [*yachal*] in him" (Job 13:15 NIV). The Message states: "Because even if he killed me, I'd keep on hoping."

This expression is one of utter confidence and dependence. This confidence does not require any understanding of what is happening. The one looked to is God and the context is one of expectation that He will respond in time of trouble. Declarations from the NIV:

*Why, my soul, are you downcast? Why so disturbed within me? Put your hope in God, for I will yet praise him, my Savior and my God.*

Psalms 42:5

*Remember your word to your servant, for you have given me hope [literally, 'made me to hope in you'].*

Psalms 119:49

*You are my refuge and shield; I have put my hope in your word.*

Psalms 119:114

In all of these Scriptures the Hebrew verb translated as "put hope in" is *yachal*. In the times that *yachal* is translated as "wait," hope could easily be substituted. Psalm 38:15 (NIV) states, "Lord, I wait [*yachal*] for you; you will answer, Lord my God."

The Hebrew word *towcheleth* from the root word, *yachal,* may be used as a general term for hope.

> *Towcheleth* (tō•kheh'•leth 6 times) Hope; General use connected to both positive and negative issues. (Strong's H8431)

*Hope deferred makes the heart sick, but a longing fulfilled is a tree of life.*

Proverbs 13:12 (NIV)

*But now, Lord, what do I look for? My hope is in you.*

Psalms 39:7 (NIV)

A prominent word for hope in the Old Testament is *qavah*.

Qavah (kä•vä' 53 times) To wait, to look for, to hope, expect. [Secondary meaning] To collect, bind together. (Strong's H6960)

Although similar to *yachal*, *qavah* contains a connotation of future time. Psalms 25:3 (NIV): "No one who hopes in you will ever be put to shame." Isaiah 40:30-31 (NIV): "Even youths grow tired and weary, and young men stumble and fall, but those who hope in the Lord will renew their strength." In the cases where *qavah* is translated as "wait" or "wait for" when referring to God, there is an element of expecting something to happen in the future. Psalms 40:1 (NIV): "I waited patiently for the Lord; he turned to me and heard my cry." When used as "wait," there is an idea of expectancy without any time frame. Hope is total dependence when circumstances are out of one's control.

Another Hebrew term used at times for the English word hope is *seber*(n)/*sabar*(v).

Seber/Sabar (sā'•ver 2 times, sä•var' 8 times) To expect with patience; Wait, expectancy        (Strong's H7664/H7663)

Psalms 146:5 (NIV): "Blessed are those whose help is in the God of Jacob, whose hope (*seber*) is in the Lord their God."

The final word that we need to look at in the Old Testament is *miqveh*.

> *Miqveh* (mik•veh' 12 times) Hope; Ground of hope; May be used to describe God Himself. (Strong's H4723)

> *Hope of Israel! Our only hope! Israel's last chance in this trouble*
>
> Jeremiah 14:8 MSG

> *From early on your Sanctuary was set high, a throne of glory, exalted! O God, you're the hope of Israel.*
>
> Jeremiah 17:12 (MSG)

# Appendix B

## Hope in the New Testament

There are a total of ninety occurrences of the Greek word hope as a verb or noun in the New Testament. These words basically mean to have a confident and favorable expectation towards God.

> *Elpis* (el-pees 54 times) A future time, vigorous looking forward to, warm, happy anticipation of good and favor. (Strong's G1680)
>
> (a) the happy anticipation of good (the most frequent), e.g., Titus 1:2, 1 Peter 1:21
>
> (b) the ground upon which hope is based, e.g., Acts 16:19; Colossians 1:27
>
> (c) the object upon which the hope is fixed, e.g., 1 Timothy 1:1.

Various phrases are used with the word hope in Paul's Epistles and speeches:

> (1) Acts 23:6 (NASB), the hope and resurrection of

the dead

(2) Acts 26:6-7, the hope of the promise, i.e., the fulfillment of the promise, made unto the fathers

(3) Galatians 5:5, the hope of righteousness, i.e., the believer's complete conformity to God's will

(4) Colossians 1:23, the hope of the Gospel, i.e., the hope of the fulfillment of all the promises presented in the Gospel

(5) Romans 5:2, (the) hope of the glory of God, i.e., as in Titus 2:13, the blessed hope and appearing of the glory of our great God and Savior Jesus Christ

(6) I Thessalonians 5:8, the hope of salvation, i.e., present and future salvation

(7) Ephesians 1:18, the hope of His (God's) calling, i.e., the prospect to become the manifest sons of God

(8) Ephesians 4:4, the hope of your calling, the same as (7) but regarded from the point of view of the called

(9) Titus 1:2; 3:7, the hope of eternal life, i.e., the full manifestation and realization of that life which is already the believer's possession

(10) Acts 28:20, the hope of Israel, i.e., the Messiah.

The objective and subjective uses of the word need to be distinguished; in Romans 15:4, e.g., the use is subjective. In

Ephesians 1:18; 2:12; 4:4, it is objective.

In Romans 15:13, God is spoken of as "the God of hope," i.e., He is the author, not the subject. Hope is a factor in salvation, Romans 8:24; it finds its expression in endurance under trial, I Thessalonians 1:3; it is "an anchor of the soul," staying amidst the storms of this life, Hebrews 6:18-19; it is a purifying power, "every one that hath this hope set on Him (Christ) purifieth himself, even as He is pure," 1 John 3:3 (the Apostle John's one mention of hope).

The phrase "fullness of hope," Hebrews 6:11, expresses the completeness of its activity in the soul.

Hope as a verb:

- *Elpizo* (el-pid'-zo 36 times) To expect or confide; To trust in; To rest upon; To wait; To rely upon. (Strong's G1679)

Biblical record exists at least in part to be a source of hope in our present experience. Romans 15:4 (NIV): "For everything that was written in the past was written to teach us, so that through endurance taught in the Scriptures and the encouragement they provide, we might have hope." The foundation established in the Old Testament expression of hope becomes manifest in the opportunity to experience hope more fully in Jesus Christ. Hebrews 7:19 (AMP): "For the Law never made anything perfect–but instead a better hope is introduced through which we [now] come close to God."

A Greek verb *apekdechomai* is not translated into hope as such but has a close association in the practical outworking of Biblical hope. (Strong's G553)

*Apekdechomai** (äp-ek-de'-kho-mī 14 times) Assiduously and patiently waiting for; Tirelessly, unremittingly, persistently expecting fully; look for; wait for.

*But if we hope for what we do not see, with perseverance we wait* eagerly* for it.*

Romans 8:25 (NASB)

*For we through the Spirit, by faith, are waiting* for the hope of righteousness.*

Galatians 5:5 (NASB)

# Appendix C

## Increase Hope Foundation

## www.IncreaseHope.com

There is always hope. Obviously, everyone does not experience hope all of the time. There is plenty of hope for everyone but often individuals need help finding a source of hope. As we give hope away, hope is increased both in our life as well as in those we give to. This book was written to increase the understanding of hope as well as discover ways to facilitate the flow of hope into the lives of others.

One current, primary focus is education. We have developed a hope building seminar: **Hope Accelerator.** This Seminar is focused on the application of teaching from the *Authentic Hope* book. A DVD series and Guide Book are currently in the development stages. As the publisher of *Authentic Hope*, www.AuthenticHopeBook.com proceeds of the sales fund the Increase Hope Foundation.

The goal of the Foundation is to select, develop and fund specific hope building endeavors. One of various concerns is the suicidal thinking that pulls people toward a dark end. A very high percentage of people have considered suicide as a way to move out of difficult, painful life situations. Notably, suicide is the second leading cause of death in 15-29 year-olds globally. For every successful attempt, some researchers estimate there are 25 unsuccessful attempts and many others who think about it without action. Increase Hope Foundation intends to be part of the community addressing this and other issues that limit the quality of life.

The Foundation is being established as a non-profit, charitable organization under the IRS 501(c)3 code. Donations to Increase Hope Foundation will be tax deductible. If you would like to join us in funding hope building endeavors, there are a variety of ways to give.

Thank you for reading *Authentic Hope*! Please join us to increase the hope flow *in possessing the unfolding future.*

# Further Information

If you would like more information on this or any other subject, feel free to contact Arnold at: www.IncreaseHope.com. Our staff will be pleased to assist you.

Look for the soon release of author-read audio book, plus DVD *Hope Accelerator Seminar* with interactive Hope Development Guide